Antlers

A Guide to Collecting, Scoring, Mounting, and Carving

DENNIS WALROD

STACKPOLE BOOKS

Published by
STACKPOLE BOOKS
5067 Ritter Rd.
Mechanicsburg, PA 17055
www.stackpolebooks.com

Printed in the United States of America

First edition

10 9 8 7 6 5 4 3 2

Cover design by Wendy A. Reynolds

Cover photograph by Jim Roach

All photographs by the author except as follows: 5, 9, 11, 12, 17: Anthony Bubenik; 22: Brown Brothers; 24: Jim Roach; 26: Jackson Hole Chamber of Commerce; 30: www.antler-sunlimited.com; 33: www.antlerdesigns.com; 41, 49: Tammy Coleman; 43, 51, 52: Doug Coleman; 56, 77–79, 174: Boone and Crockett Club; 59, 177, 179: Ohio Whitetail Hall of Fame; 62, 186: Deerassic Park; 99 (top and bottom): McKenzie Taxidermy Supply, Inc.; 110: Glen Conley; 112 (top and bottom): Larry Blomquist; 115: Gary Bowen; 121: Jack Brown; 131 (top): Foredom Tool Company; 131 (bottom), 157: Larry Baesler; 146: Eric Carr; 158: Shane Wilson; 160: Ayal Hausfeld; 166: Stanley Hill

For more on antlers, hunting, and wildlife management, check out www.denniswalrod.com.

Library of Congress Cataloguing-in-Publication Data

Walrod, Dennis.
    Antlers : a guide to collecting, scoring, mounting, and carving / Dennis Walrod.
        p. cm.
    ISBN-13: 978-0-8117-3229-1
    ISBN-10: 0-8117-3229-0
    1. Antlers. I. Title.

QL942.W35 2005
799.2'765—dc22
                                        2005016903

To Justin, Christopher, Ashlee,
Ryan, Chelsea, and Ethan,
who do not yet know who they are
nor what they can become

CONTENTS

ACKNOWLEDGMENTS

Wow, writing the acknowledgments for this book is tough work! There are so many significant contributors that I have to wonder whether just my name or all of theirs together should appear under the title. *Antlers* is a book that wanted to be written . . . or probably more accurately, that all of these people wanted to be written, to serve as a central resource for their varied antler-related interests.

Several times, as my publication deadlines loomed, unexpected insights and information were revealed that required me to change the direction the book was taking. I had just finished another book, *Making the Most of Your Deer*, when Brant Davis, owner of Wild Creations in Ellicottville, New York, told me that if I was truly interested in doing a book about antlers, I absolutely had to visit Lenny Nagel at his Antler Shed. So I did, and viewed thousands of whitetail antlers and learned about developments in their dollar value . . . and if I didn't believe Len, I could look it up on eBay.

Well, I didn't, so I did. Look it up on eBay, that is, and that's where I met Jack Brown, the "Bonecarver," whom I later visited a hundred miles down the pike in Wellsville, New York. In his antler store, Brown told me about the commissioned carving he was doing for Deerassic Park, a place in Ohio that I would have to see for myself. So I traveled there to talk with Dean Ziegler, the founder of the National Whitetail Deer Education Foundation, the programs of which will influence the way many people will think about antlers in the future.

Somewhere along in there I did an online search for the possible existence of antler-related books like the one I wanted to write. I didn't find any, but I did locate an antler-science publication edited by Dr. George Bubenik of Ontario, Canada, whom I then asked for advice and help. Virtually all of the scientific observations and data that are included here were cheerfully provided by this world-renowned antler researcher, zoology professor, and M.D., or were published earlier by his late father, Dr. Anthony Bubenik, who was an antler researcher and—as you can see in the several illustrations by him that are in this book—a talented artist. Larry Blomquist, editor of *Breakthrough* taxidermy magazine, supplied photos, procedures for making replicas of antlers, and estimates of the current values of trophy antlers as graphed in Chapter 2. Which reminds me, thanks also to the Boone and Crockett Club, particularly the director of publications, Julie Houk, who provided me with access to the trophy database that I used to plot several national trends in antler size and type.

Contributing wildlife artists, including graphic artists, sculptors, artisans, and taxidermists whose works or techniques are displayed in this book were Dr. Anthony Bubenik, Larry Baesler, Paul Blum, Gary Bowen, Eric Carr, Glen Conley, Tim Ferrie, Ayal Hausfeld, Wayne Henry, Russell Hill, Cole Johnson, Paul Luczah, Earl Martz, Evelyn Maryanski, Jack Paluh, Mat Snyder, Shane Wilson, and Bill Yox.

A method for training dogs to search for shed antlers was kindly provided by Tammy Coleman. Marilyn Erickson helped me numerous times to reconcile what I was trying to write with what I was actually thinking. Mike Darr explained some of the shifts in deer habitat that had occurred over time and that might have influenced trends in antler size. Deer biologist Keith McCaffery steered me down a different fork in the road just when I needed a fresh perspective on what this antler-culture phenomenon is all about, and where it might be going. Lastly, I am deeply indebted to my Stackpole Books editor, Christopher Chappell, for hacking a clear and well-marked trail through the tangled mess of words and photographs that I sent to him.

INTRODUCTION

THE HUMAN FASCINATION
WITH ANTLERS

Over the last ten years or so, a growing segment of the general public—including people who don't hunt, who have never seen a deer in the wild, or even who don't know that deer shed their antlers every year—has gone absolutely nuts about antlers.

A new national organization, the Quality Deer Management Association, along with the wildlife management departments of several states, has begun promoting harvest guidelines designed to allow older bucks to develop larger antlers, which has also increased interest in trophy-antler hunting while keeping the excessive whitetail population under control. The National Whitetail Deer Education Foundation, which also supports the Deerassic Park Education Center in Ohio, wisely uses the fascination that humans naturally have for antlers as a carrot on a stick to focus the interest of school children on nature and the outdoors. There's a rapidly growing enthusiasm among outdoors people who search the spring woodlands for antlers dropped in late winter by live bucks, and now they're organized under the North American Shed Hunters Club, which provides an official measuring and recording system. An expression of a growing interest in trophy antlers can also be seen in the raw statistics of the Boone and Crockett Club, which has recorded far more high-scoring antler racks in the past ten years than during the entire twentieth century.

The Internet has had something to do with this by bringing people of common interests together . . . and it hasn't hurt that eBay and other sites have provided balanced buyer-seller markets where the monetary value of antlers can develop in the clear light of supply and demand. Some people cringe at the thought of the words "money" and "antlers" occurring in the same sentence, as though there might be some cheapening of our interest in the outdoors and its wildlife. It's important to remember, though, that deer are a renewable source of antlers (especially shed antlers) and that the worst enemy of our environment and its wildlife is a simple lack of interest. In fact, the increased value in America of antlers for carving and art stems in part from conservation efforts in Africa to protect the elephant population from poachers. Importation of ivory is now tightly controlled and no longer widely available to artisans, so antler bone is now often substituted . . . and a new art form has emerged, kept viable by online customers and art collectors with money in their pockets. The increased availability of shed antlers has also enabled and encouraged their use in the creation of rustic furniture and lighting fixtures that are suitable for certain high-end restaurants and country chalets.

This book covers all these aspects of antler interest, and it also includes information on antler biology and the potential of antler research for important medical breakthroughs. Last, and very definitely *least* in importance, there's even a recipe for how to cook and eat a portion of hard antler. No kidding.

A NOTE ON SPECIES
This book gives information on the antlers of all the North American cervid species: whitetail deer, mule deer, moose, caribou, and elk. In North America, only the males of the deer species have antlers, *except* the female caribou, who also has them. The five species are described in this book in detail that's roughly proportional to the percentages below. These rankings are based on the 7,022 sets of trophy antlers that were registered by the Boone and Crockett Club between 1994 and 2004. A more detailed breakdown of all these species and their subspecies, including the Tule elk and the Sitka blacktail, is shown in Chapter 4.

PERCENTAGE OF DEER SPECIES REGISTERED, BOONE AND CROCKETT CLUB, 1994–2004

Whitetail Deer 57

Mule Deer 13

Moose 12

Caribou 11

Elk 7

Wherever in this book you see the word "deer" by itself, I am referring to all five species of the deer family, unless I preface the word with "whitetail" or "mule."

1

INCREDIBLE ANTLERS

"If antlered mammals had not evolved, the existence of such improbable creatures would never have been imagined, even in the annals of science fiction."

—DR. RICHARD GOSS
PROFESSOR EMERITUS OF BIOLOGY AND MEDICINE
BROWN UNIVERSITY

HEY, DEER . . . THERE'S A LEG GROWING OUT OF YOUR HEAD! We all know that antlers are not just figments of a science fiction writer's imagination, but the reality of these marvelous appendages is still absolutely incredible. Yes, an antler is very much like an actual "leg" growing out of a deer's head. The only difference is that an antler has neither muscles nor joints for movement. In spring and summer, the growing velvet antler has a complex internal vein-and-artery structure within the dense marrow of the developing bone, a network of nerves that extends all the way to the tips of the tines, and a covering of skin with true hair and oil glands. The growing antler would feel warm to your touch . . . a touch that a buck would be able to feel and attempt to avoid. If you were to forcibly saw off a velvet antler, the deer would feel great pain and could even bleed to death.

(A warning: if you think details like these are surprising, the insights that follow will be so much more enlightening, the truths so glaringly different from what you might have believed, that at this point I almost feel impelled to advise you to put this book down and read no further. If you don't, you'll never see antlers the same way you do now.)

While still a fawn, a male deer is not yet capable of growing antlers. He's born with a thin layer of connective tissue called the antlerogenic periosteum tucked under the skin on the front surface of his skull. During the onset of puberty about four months later, a surge of testosterone

Velvet antlers are the fastest-growing appendages in the animal kingdom. The mysteries of that rapid growth and annual regeneration are being seriously studied by modern scientists for potential benefits to human health and well-being.

causes the growth of two bony bumps called pedicles, which serve as the platforms for future antler development. Tiny antler buttons, which in the case of the whitetail and mule deer are hardly the size of small acorns, begin growing from the pedicles later in summer, and it's not until the following summer that larger shapes that we'd recognize as "spike" antlers are grown. Each winter, the existing antlers are shed, and by early the following summer, the regeneration of new antlers begins anew.

If at any time a tiny piece of the antlerogenic tissue were to be cut out and transplanted elsewhere on the deer's skin, a small antler would begin to grow there the next summer. It wouldn't get very big and it definitely wouldn't be something you'd ever call a trophy, but it would be, for sure, an antler. Under controlled clinical conditions, such "antlers" have successfully been grown on deer's ears, near their eyes, and out of their shoulders and legs.

What comes next really does seem to enter into the realm of science fiction. If that tiny piece of embryonic antler stem-cell material is embedded instead on a mouse's head, a tiny bump of an antler will grow there too. This has been done by medical scientists, photographed, and published—not in the supermarket tabloids, but in learned professional journals. To my knowledge, none of the scientists have dared say that this would work with humans . . . but if a mouse can reliably grow deer antlers, would you doubt that humans could do it, too? The human race has such an abundance of tattooed-and-pierced wonders, bungee-jumpers, sky-divers, extreme skiers, and other similarly, um, culturally advanced people that it surely wouldn't be difficult to find volunteers for an experiment. The only real difficulty would be, I think, in telling the unsuccessful applicants that they had to leave and go home. Probably, the scientists would eventually have to call the police.

Testosterone is the essential steroid involved in the regulation of the antler cycle, beginning with the initiation of growth and followed by rapid development. In large-antlered deer (meaning elk, moose, and caribou), the velvet antler can grow as rapidly as 2 centimeters (about $3/4$ inch) per day, which is almost as fast as stalks of corn grow on a warm summer day after a rainfall. Ultimately, some of the testosterone is converted to estrogen, which causes the death of the velvet and the mineralization of the antler to hard bone. After the deer rubs off the dried and sometimes bloody velvet, its antlers are revealed to be bones growing out of its head—just bare bones, sort of like a serious compound fracture that just wouldn't stop healing.

Once you accept this, you might begin wondering how the antler knows to grow into nearly the same forks and tines as it did the previous year, only bigger and more impressive. Get this: of all the mammals on the face of the earth, deer are the only ones that can regenerate a complete organ. Sure, a lizard can regrow a leg or a stumpy tail-of-sorts if you cut the original one off, but no warm-blooded mammal can do that. A buck deer, however, can regenerate the "leg" of an antler year after year; it usually becomes bigger and better with each new growth until advancing age converts length into thickness. This amazing capability is a major reason that so much advanced research is being done on antlers. Antler research for medical applications in humans has increased greatly in recent years, paralleling the advent of stem cell research. An extract made from the growing velvet antler tip has successfully been used by Canadian scientists for bone grafts in laboratory mice. Taking this one step further, it's now been determined that the structure of fresh antler is very similar to human bones and would possibly be effective for reconstructive surgery. (See Chapter 5 for more details.)

The antlers themselves don't die when the buck rubs off the velvet but, in fact, remain viable for several months, usually right up to the time that they are dropped. (Mounted trophy antlers and old sheds, on the other hand, are relatively brittle and need to be handled carefully.) This hasn't been known for very long, but it makes sense: because bucks use their polished antlers for tests of strength against other bucks, it's important that they retain some resiliency and impact resistance. The relevant studies have been conducted mainly on European fallow deer, but the results are applicable to the other deer species as well, according to researchers. Capillaries and blood vessels provide a rich supply of moisture and nutrients to the otherwise dense "marrow" of the main beam as well as the harder antler bone surrounding it. In one deer that had rubbed its velvet off three months earlier, researchers even found living bone cells reproducing within the antler core, plus evidence that suggested diffusion of blood within the porous inner structure of the antler, a full 18 inches from the buck's skull. Like teeth or elephant tusks, antlers are in a sort of "suspended animation," metabolically speaking.

Nonetheless, hard antlers have no "feeling"—the nerves themselves have ceased to function. Otherwise, battling other bucks would hurt!

An important note: *antlers are not horns!* Horns have a bony core that protrudes from the skull and is covered by keratin, the same stuff from which hooves and claws are made. Horns usually grow on both sexes of the bovids (cattle, sheep, goats, and so on). Horns are never shed, and if they're cut off, they will never grow back.

TINES, FORKS, BEAMS, AND MORE

Being the antler fanatics that we are (yeah . . . I'm talkin' to *you*!), we should agree what we're going to call the various parts of antlers. Of course, as you already know, the characteristic antler shapes of each of the five main species are different from all the others, and one of them (the whitetail's) probably exhibits more variation than the others combined, with the potential, apparently, to produce an unlimited number of tines. In comparison, it seems that elk antlers come in only a few standard styles, and for a bull of a given age and size, you'll almost always find the proscribed number of tines in the expected places.

The butt-end of an antler where it attaches to the skull is called the *seal*, and it is immediately rimmed by the *coronet*, which flares out from the antler as though to keep the hide tightly affixed to the skull. The *shaft* begins at the coronet; for a few inches (and sometimes considerably more) above the coronet it is covered by a rough surface called the *burr* (not shown in the illustration) on which can often be found small *pearls* that look like large droplets of wax dripping down the side of a candle. The main *beam* includes the shaft and is the longest portion of

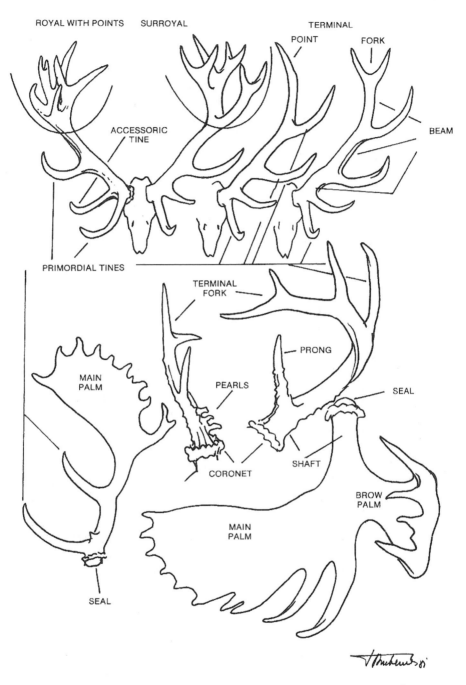

ROYAL WITH POINTS   SURROYAL

TERMINAL

POINT   FORK

ACCESSORIC
TINE

BEAM

PRIMORDIAL TINES

TERMINAL
FORK

PRONG

MAIN
PALM

PEARLS

SEAL

SHAFT

CORONET

BROW
PALM

MAIN
PALM

SEAL

The terminology of antlers is the same for carvers and sculptors as it is for collectors and trophy hunters.

the antlers. The *tines* sprout from the main beam. Those first-appearing tines that are closest to the skull are most commonly referred to as *brow tines, prongs,* or *eye guards.* A tine or main beam can end at a *fork,* which is a major characteristic of the mule deer. Note that although the conjunction of the main beam and the farthest tine on a whitetail antler might appear to be a fork, it technically isn't unless the balance of that fork is more like a "Y" than an "L." (If it actually is a "Y," the offending tine will be scored by the Boone and Crockett Club either as a negative or a "non-typical.")

As mentioned earlier, elk tines develop in a very regular pattern, allowing each tine to have its own special name. Beginning with the one closest to the skull, the tines are called 1) *brow,* 2) *bez,* 3) *trez,* 4) *dagger,* 5) *fifth* (yes, "fifth"), and, at the end of the main beam, 6) *royal.* Sometimes, if you're especially lucky, there will be a *surroyal,* which may have additional small points of its own. Moose antlers and portions of caribou antlers have characteristic *palms* and *brow palms,* but any of the five species of North America can sometimes have minor flattened areas that would be described by insiders (which now includes you) as being "palmated."

BIZARRE ANTLERS

Injury to any place on a deer's body, not just the antlers, will often cause the growth of freakish antlers to occur the following year . . . but only if the deer gets a chance to think about it. (Here we go again, plunging off into what must seem to be like science fiction!) If a deer in the wild is wounded on its left hip, for example, but survives to grow antlers the following year, the antler on the other side, the right side, will be deformed and usually smaller. All the details won't be clear enough yet to predict just what the deformity will be, but what is fairly well documented is that it will persist for additional years of antler regrowth.

This in itself is amazing, but the established prediction of abnormality bounces over the curb and spins out on the grass of the truly weird when the injury is instead applied under an anesthetic, such as in surgery. If a buck's left leg is carefully amputated while he's sedated, the next year's right antler will still be the same as the left one; nothing will have changed except the number of the deer's legs.

So . . . why? Well, we know that in all mammals, one side of the body is controlled by the other side of the brain, so the deformation of an opposing antler doesn't really stretch our imagination too much.

Still, the apparent necessity for the sensation of pain to cause an opposing antler deformity implies that the deer's brain has some unconscious neurological control over how an antler will grow; it's not just at the basic cellular level of programming. That's amazing. Still, no self-respecting scientist with a career to protect would ever go so far as to suggest, in this decade at least, that a deer's brain could voluntarily control the growth of a "leg" out of its head. Even I, beholden to no one except my editor, hesitate to suggest that since a mouse can grow antlers and so maybe we humans can, too, that the mechanism by which you and I could control the regeneration of a lost limb . . . might be in our heads already?

Still, consider this: if a buck is defeated in a skirmish during the rutting season, the following summer his ability to grow antlers will be impaired, and by the next rutting season, his rack will usually be significantly smaller. This tells us that what's going on inside a deer's brain (his "self-esteem"?) has more effect on the antlers on his head than science has yet been able to grasp. It also illustrates just one more reason why antler research may open doors to a better understanding of human health.

INJURY TO THE VELVET ANTLER

A growing velvet antler is especially vulnerable to breakage and other traumas. Despite the great care that a buck takes in summer to avoid bumping into anything with his tender antlers, accidents can happen—such as right-of-way conflicts with automobiles. Sometimes a fragile antler can fracture but be held at a bent angle by the skin, like a broken candy cane in its plastic wrapper. If the blood supply isn't disrupted, both broken ends can continue to develop and even reconnect. If they do, the antler when fully developed will display an abrupt downward bend where the fracture occurred. If the healing process fails to bring the two broken ends together, the broken end will fall to the ground when the velvet dies, even though it might have been nourished all along by a steady blood supply. This leaves a stub-like cross-section on the original antler that often reveals the rounded signs of partial healing. Sometimes an accident causes only a crack in the core of the velvet antler, and the effects of healing will be manifested in the hard antler as only a swelling in the region of the crack.

If the base pedicle itself is damaged before an antler has had a chance to begin growing, a smaller accessory antler may begin to grow either from the original location of the pedicle or somewhere closely adjacent to it. There's a shed whitetail antler on my desk that has a deeply grooved area on the underside of the main beam that briefly flares outward, almost like a minor palmation; I suspect that the velvet core had at one point been cracked lengthwise.

Injury or stress to the developing velvet antler (not the deer's body) can also result in what is known as hypertrophic growth, resulting in a bizarre shape and massive size. George Bubenik, who is also a professor of zoology at the University of Guelph, Ontario, has been trying to find out why this happens. Take a look at the illustrations on the following page, which track three years of antler development on "Billy," a pen-raised buck. (These sketches were done by the late Dr. Anthony Bubenik, George's father, who was himself an antler researcher as well as an obviously talented artist.)

Billy-the-buck was a normal six-point buck at age two, but the following summer, he accidentally split the velvet bud on his right side and went on to produce *two* main beams on *both* sides of his head. Somehow, the trauma of the first injury was shared equally on both sides. The year after that, he had the standard one beam per side, one with six points and the other with a split at the brow tine. At age five, another accident resulted in injury, again to his right velvet bud, and that autumn he was sporting hugely hypertrophic antlers that, when shed, together weighed over eleven pounds. A year later, Billy again had enormous antlers on both sides, even though the original injuries had been on the same side. Then he damaged the left pedicle to the point of actually ripping out a piece of the skull, which resulted in a stunted antler as shown in the sketch. Full regeneration of the pedicle by the next year resulted in a return of the large malformed antlers on both sides.

Why did Billy's antlers grow to such great sizes, and how did injury on one side get communicated and transferred to the other side? On the matter of size, George Bubenik hypothesized that possible injury to the nerves of the pedicle had over-stimulated the growth rate. He later tested this possibility by applying a mild but constant direct electrical current (DC) to stimulate the nerves of growing mule deer antlers. The resulting antlers were stunted and misshapen. However, the application of alternating current (AC) resulted in a 70 percent increase in antler length and a 40 percent weight gain. In subsequent years of no treatment, the antlers reverted to their normal size. This left the physical pain of the original accidental injury as a possible cause of Billy's exuberant growths. This was before it was found that purposeful damage to the velvet antlers of anesthetized deer did not result in hypertrophic antler development.

a

b

c

Injury to one side of a deer's forehead or to a single, developing velvet antler often results in grotesque developments of both antlers for some years afterward.

I'm leaving out a whole bunch of highly technical stuff here, plus the details of several other experiments that were conducted on the role of the nerves and brain function in velvet development. (This is partly because I don't fully understand them.) But what I do gather is that antlers are far more mysterious than even a science-fiction writer could ever have imagined. George Bubenik believes that the massive antler growths following velvet injuries may indicate that there is great potential for bucks in the wild to produce larger antlers than have been seen so far. Of course, there is also a genetic component to antler growth, as is demonstrated by the "super antlers" sometimes produced on deer farms. I personally wonder about the extent to which the impressive antlers of farm-raised deer are solely the product of selective breeding, rather than the outcome of bucks injuring their velvet antlers on the metal fences around them.

ANTLERS AND AERODYNAMICS

Antlered deer are always very much aware, even when running at full speed, how close they can come to a tree without snagging it. They learned this avoidance behavior earlier when their antlers were in velvet and the nerves were still alive. The feeling of the wind passing through their developing rack helped them to learn the positions of their antlers, even though they couldn't see them. The soft fuzz on the velvet, being real hair, probably aided in this awareness. Through measured observation by wildlife biologists, it's been found that deer also become familiar with their antlers from practicing sparring with bushes and tree limbs, and that they're able to bring their outer points within an inch and a half of making contact with anything. Deer also gently groom their velvet antlers with their hind hooves, at least partly to keep the velvet well-groomed and cover it with pheromones from the oil glands.

Once the antlers have been mineralized to near-solid bone, however, the buck has to rely on unconscious memory, just as we do when parallel-parking a car in a tight space. For the five deer species of this book, those parking spaces come in many different sizes and dimensions. The extreme diversity of antler shapes found among deer species is partly due to adaptations to the various habitats in which they live.

The whitetail deer thrives in thick, brushy thickets—so thick that you or I would have to get down on our hands and knees just to crawl along their trails—and in tall-grass meadows and young woodlands where the saplings and wild berry canes grow so close together that carrying even a garden rake would be a struggle. A typical whitetail buck, though, can virtually glide right through all that stuff by utilizing the inwardly curved, horizontal main beams and tines of his plow-shaped rack. The rack works like the rounded front bumpers on an ATV: where vines and overhanging braches might otherwise scratch the deer's eyes and ears, the tines neatly comb though the stringy obstacles and guide them over the main beams . . . all at top speed, if necessary.

Elk, caribou, and moose, all generally being creatures of more open areas, rely on their oversized antlers in part for long-distance connection and recognition. In the tundra and open prairie, though, the constant force of the blowing wind can exact a price for that communication. When the wind is really ripping, the high antlers of the barren ground caribou force the male to travel either with or against the direction of the wind. The adaptation here is that the barren ground caribou has more aerodynamically shaped "paddles" at the top of its antlers and over the bridge of its nose, whereas the more sheltered woodland caribou can afford to have a less obscured face and wider and more extravagant

For protection against the strong winds that blow in the open regions, the barren ground caribou (top right) *carries aerodynamic antlers that offer less resistance. The wind-sheltered habitat of the woodland caribou* (lower left) *provides more opportunity for the lavish development of more complex antlers.*

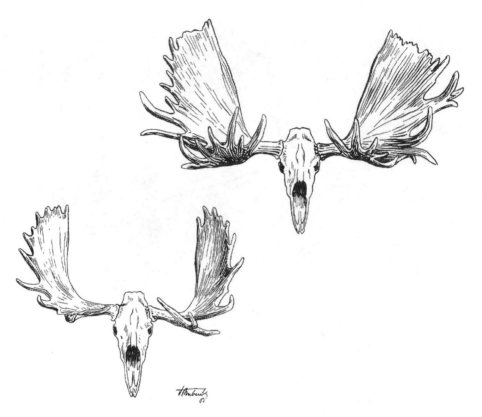

Antlers are adapted to the habitats in which they develop. The wide-spread antlers of the tundra moose (top right) are cup-shaped in a way that is aerodynamically "uplifting." In comparison, the woodland moose (lower left) contends with the obstacles of trees and close-growing brush; consequently, the bull's wide palms are turned sideways for easier passage.

antlers that are held high in the sky. Elk, on the other hand, have antlers that are swept back, enabling the bull to lower resistance just by raising his head and nose, which aligns the antlers into a streamlined fashion close to his back.

Moose come in two basic designs, too, but in aerodynamically different ways. You would expect that a tundra moose holding his wide-spread antlers broadside to a stiff wind would feel a strong resistance to forward movement, but that apparently doesn't happen. Experiments performed with antler dummies (described later in this chapter) have indicated that the aerodynamics of the antler's upturned "cup" actually seem to lighten the heavy load. On the other hand, the woodland moose lives where the wind doesn't blow as hard but where there are trees and bushes to walk between, and the broad palms are partially turned so as to shorten the "wingspan," with only a minor loss in aerodynamics.

ANTLERS AS WEAPONS

Antlers are not ordinarily used by deer for killing or injuring. If they had been intended for serious bloodletting, they would need to have been designed somewhat differently—more like swords than garden rakes. Of course, to the human eye, the antlers of the whitetail deer, mule deer, elk, caribou, and moose appear fearsome and deadly, and you certainly wouldn't ever want to fall down a flight of stairs carrying an armload of any of them.

Consider instead, though, the circumstance of two whitetail bucks going at it head-to-head in a contest to establish who-gets-to-take-her-home superiority. With their heads both down, the bucks' sharp tines are directed horizontally toward each other. However, their long main beams are almost perpendicular to the ground, allowing them to serve almost like the safety hilt of a knife. Yes, the menacing tines could still seriously pierce the body of the other deer if the antler rack were abruptly pushed forward, which is easy for us to imagine. However, such an action would be difficult for the deer to perform short of throwing its entire body forward with a leap off the rear feet. Unlike a Holstein bull that can stab, rip, and gore with its curved horns simply by thrusting its head to one side, deer can literally only scratch the surface.

Sometimes accidents do happen where serious injury leads to the death of a buck, but these events usually occur in fenced-in areas or high-population regions where stress levels are high and the loser can't escape. When healthy deer engage in a battle, their antlers are used mostly as a sort of "mechanical connector" that allows them to engage in a relatively harmless series of pushing contests. The various tines are well placed to protect a buck's eyes and face, and the main beams protect the throat and neck. The younger bucks, with their narrow sets of spikes and fork-horn antlers, can actually be more dangerous to a larger buck because the two racks don't lock together. But most often, a look at the relative size of an older adversary's antlers is enough to convince smaller bucks that the battle just wouldn't be worth the effort.

Overall, the visual display of antlers and the pre-fighting rituals and casual sparring are usually more important than the fight itself. It's now known that sparring skills and the ability to "read" the opposition are not instinctual but are learned during these preliminary activities.

ANTLERS FOR COMMUNICATING

We tend to think of the males of the deer species as behaving all year long as though their antlers never fell off in late winter. But fall they do, and all the rituals and posturing disappear during the months of spring and early summer, when male and female alike are effectively neutered by the decline of their sex hormones. Then, as the days of early summer begin, there's a hormonal shift that begins another year of antler growth, though the deer's behavior does not change back right away.

Deer grow new antlers each year for the singular purpose of procreation. The size and condition of a buck's antlers are representative of his maturity, physical health, and social standing in the herd. In other words, his DNA, and his potential for producing similarly strong and healthy offspring, can largely be determined from the appearance of the antlers he wears. So their appearance is important to the seduction of the females, who (by the way) are the ones that make the ultimate selection with whom to mate.

Beyond this, antlers serve other purposes related to mating in the short months leading up to the rut. These involve their abilities to transmit scent, produce sound, and provide visual cues.

Scent is produced by the sebaceous (oil) glands of velvet antlers. All mammals have sebaceous glands for the general purpose of keeping the skin soft and supple. On a buck, the number of antler oil glands per square inch is greater than on any other place on its body. The scent is probably of a hormonal sort, most likely involving pheromones.

As the buck travels through the woods, the height and relatively large surface area of his antlers helps disperse the scent into the air. As if this were not enough, he will also rub his antlers over his body, including some or all of the glands on his lower body—the better to spread the good news that he is *here*! Although the breeding season hasn't begun yet, the self-promotion begins early. As with most animal scents, the identity of a buck as a specific individual probably becomes established at this point, and the females can become accustomed to his favorite routes for traveling.

Now, fast-forwarding to the time when the buck is rutting and the female is in estrus (and the contests have been won over other bucks), the female will still want one last whiff of antler scent before agreeing to breed. Having seen the buck's antlers and having been duly impressed, she still needs to establish that he is a male of her species and not just a tree or an archery dummy-target. By this time the velvet will have dried and been rubbed from the hard antler, but surely some scent will still remain. To ensure that his identity as a male is maintained and that there's no slack in his pheromonal advertising, a buck may also urinate directly on his antlers or on low-lying bushes that he can then rub his antlers in. Such is the price of love.

Sounds emanating loudly from the antlers of two bucks battling each other can be heard over long distances, attracting other bucks who might want to check out the competition and maybe even jump into the fray themselves. According to popular lore, these distant bucks figure that with all those sounds of antlers being slammed forcefully together, there must be at least one female in heat close to the action. Deer hunters often attempt to duplicate this woodland drama by "rattling" two antlers together, and sometimes they've been successful . . . but not often.

Until recently, there has been little or no actual proof that the bucks that came in to take a look were actually attracted by the sounds of rattling or just happened to be walking through the neighborhood. Technology applied by a team of wildlife biologists on the King Ranch in Texas has finally shown that rattling not only works, it turns out to be roughly three times more effective than even the most optimistic hunters had thought. In the three-year study, 130 whitetail bucks of all ages were radio-collared, including 43 bucks that wore motion-sensitive devices that informed the researchers whether the bucks were bedded down or were moving. The researchers also characterized each buck by age and antler measurements and gave each of them a unique radio frequency for purposes of identification.

Then the actual "rattling" stage of the study began. Once a buck had been located in the thick brush via its radio transmitter, the researchers would hide within 200 to 300 yards upwind of the deer and then begin banging two antlers together to make loud cracking and grinding noises. All in all, according to the motion-detector devices, nearly 75 percent of these bucks got up off their beds and came toward the sound made by the hidden rattlers. Of these bucks, 60 percent approached from downwind, meaning that they had sneaked around the rattlers in order to sniff the wind before approaching more closely. A particularly interesting thing about this study is that a mere 45 percent of the approaching bucks were ever actually seen; the others were betrayed only by their radio transmitters. But the fact is, rattling works, and during the rut, bucks really do respond to the sounds of antlers clashing together.

There was yet another fascinating discovery that came out of this study, one that related to the size of the surveyed bucks' antlers . . . but before we check it out, take a guess right now as to whether the older bucks with bigger racks were more inclined or less inclined to leave their hidden beds to approach the sound of rattling. It would make sense that the older and presumably wiser and more experienced bucks would prefer to remain where they were, in hiding, right? Right? Nope. Whereas two-thirds of the trophy-class bucks scoring 130 inches or higher succumbed to the siren call of rattling, just half of the smaller bucks moved toward the sounds of possible sexual opportunity. Knowing this now, we can hypothesize that the bigger whitetail bucks wanted to investigate the apparent trespassing of other bucks onto their private turf, and, consistent with this, that the smaller bucks weren't as eager to cause any trouble that might result in their getting knocked flat on their butts. My own take is that when you get older, it's often far better to rise out of bed when you hear opportunity knocking than to stay there and just daydream about it.

You have to wonder . . . would these bucks have responded as enthusiastically to the sounds of, say, an antler whacking against a galvanized metal gate? Good question. According to Bill Yox, a deer farmer, whitetail expert, and contributor to the taxidermy magazine *Breakthrough*, some of his fenced-in bucks will loudly rake their antlers again and again over the struts of their metal gates during the rut. Then, suddenly, they'll stop and look for several moments at one or another buck in their distant pastures as if to say, "Betcha can't do any better than that!" There's no science to this observation, but it seems reasonably clear that bucks during the rut like to make a lot of noise with their antlers so that other bucks will be impressed.

Seeing antlers at a distance is an important way for the deer species to recognize each other when the wind is blowing in a direction that doesn't allow for scenting. Actually, deer aren't too handy at seeing much of anything except movement and certain easily recognizable shapes, such as the antlers of their own species. Deer's eyes are located along the sides of their heads, unlike those of predators (including we humans), which are frontally located—"the better to see you with," as the wolf once said from Grandmother's bed. This causes them to have poor stereoscopic vision, meaning they don't have much depth perception. Consequently, when a deer sees another deer head-on or even from the rear end, they can't tell whether it is coming or going. If the deer displays a rump patch—such as the flared white tail of the whitetail deer—the observing deer just sees it as an undistinguished part of the "whole" deer. The point is, none of the deer species can count legs. From the front, they "see" only the neck and antlers, and they don't care about the body that connects the front to the rear. So, they need to have specific patterns to recognize during the breeding season, a role that antlers fill.

This was cleverly demonstrated in the field by the late Dr. Anthony Bubenik, who, while disguised with dummy antlers of the appropriate species mounted on a sculptured Styrofoam head, was several times able to lure wild bull moose, bull elk, and caribou bulls to within 50 yards or less. He brought a shy, high-fenced European red deer stag (an elk subspecies) to within nose-to-nose range. Bubenik made no attempt to hide the fact of his human scent or that he was walking on only two legs with no deer body behind him. Yet, he was able to skillfully communicate with the approaching deer by carefully mimicking the ritualized neck, head, and antler postures and movements that are understood only by other deer of the same species. The body language—no, make that the *antler* language—of deer is precise, complex, and different for each of the species. In all cases, Bubenik was able to "talk" his way out of potentially serious and dangerously one-sided skirmishes. With one particular caribou that was inclined to attack

With large-antlered deer such as the elk, moose, and caribou, just the sight of antlers can override the bull's fear of human scent and cause it to ignore the lesser number of legs underneath them.

aggressively, Bubenik could stop the bull in his tracks by swerving the dummy antlers in such a way that a real caribou would never do. Then, when he again made a correct display, the bull would immediately repeat his attack.

When Bubenik encountered elk, they became suspicious of the obvious human scent he emitted from his antlered masquerade, but they held their ground. The barren ground caribou were even less concerned about the human scent and actually searched for the human form behind the dummy. The moose were so focused on the antlers that they completely ignored the scent. Note the trend in antler size here: the most suspicious species of the three was the elk, with the smallest antlers, and the least suspicious was the moose, with the largest. All three tend to live in open areas where long-range vision is possible. The tundra moose can communicate to other bulls over distances of a mile or more just by bobbing his head in their direction, which results in a sort of strobe-lighting effect as the sun reflects off of the palmated antlers. Knowing this, you can better understand why, compared to the other species, moose would be more influenced by antlers than human odor.

On the other hand, the whitetail deer, the deer species with the smallest antlers, lives in cover that's often so thick and tangled that a "long-range" view might be all of a few short yards. If Anthony Bubenik's suggested formula—larger antlers indicating advanced reliance on optical recognition at long ranges—can be extrapolated downward, then we wouldn't expect whitetail bucks to be suckered by a two-legged set of antlers that smelled like a human. (Limited studies were done by Bubenik's staff on pen-raised deer, but the only response was curiosity. No further studies were done on the subject.) Still, as a hunter, I'm interested in this for at least two reasons. I wonder if whitetail bucks could be brought into closer range by the use of a decoy made just of antlers and perhaps a head—and if they could, whether that decoy would be just as effective if it were just cut out of a flat board and painted, since the stereoscopic vision of a whitetail is no better than the rest of the species. (A flat decoy would be safer to use in woods where other hunters were looking for the same thing.)

I started thinking about this several years ago when an archery-hunter friend of mine, Dick Thayer, told me the story about how he'd been attacked by a whitetail buck. Here's how it went: The sun had gone down and Dick was late getting out of the woods. As he approached the edge of an overgrown field in thick goldenrod, Dick had to raise his compound bow high in front of him to avoid getting snagged. Suddenly a buck appeared in the trail just a few yards ahead, looking intently elsewhere . . . and then it saw Dick, whirled toward him, and charged. In that brief instant, Dick defensively shoved the bow down on the buck's antlers as he jumped sideways into the now darkened woods. End of story—the buck disappeared, and Dick found his bow and sang loudly all the way back to his pickup. Could it be that the buck momentarily mistook the uplifted compound bow for a set of antlers—and became so fixated by the visual cue that it ignored all evidence to the contrary? I think so. I have also read that American Indians were able to closely approach deer by impersonating them by wearing a buckskin and a set of antlers.

FEMALE RESPONSES AND PREFERENCES

These many daring experiments by Anthony Bubenik provided additional insights into what antlers mean to the various deer species that wear them . . . and to the females that observe them. In the potentially sensitive matter of whether size matters, there are two correct answers. One of them is Yes. The other is No. That's right, and I'm not kidding. In all the dummy tests with fake elk, caribou, and moose antlers of significantly different sizes, all the females were invariably more enamored with large antlers than the smaller ones. Female moose and caribou appeared particularly eager to switch to the dummy if it wore larger antlers than what they'd already recently settled for. Twice, moose females went wild for larger-antlered dummies and even offered themselves for copulation although they had just promised themselves to a lesser-antlered bull. (Hey, I never claimed that this would be easy reading.) On the other hand, antlers that exceed the species' socially acceptable limit, such as those sometimes seen on deer farms where the natural genetic potential can be grossly exceeded, are shunned.

Although a female in estrus is inclined to select a mate on the basis of antler size when faced with two males that are the about the same size and proper shape, she will still ultimately want to smell the antlers of both males for pheromonal information before making her final decision. In every case where this occurred with Bubenik's dummy, the dummy lost, as would any strange male that might have appeared, fought, and beaten the familiar home-grown defender. As Bubenik reported, thinking of the size of antlers as the only predictor of physical fitness is an anthropomorphic fantasy.

2

ANTLER MANIA

WHAT IS THE HUMAN EQUIVALENT OF ANTLERS?

I believe that anyone reading this book is an antler fanatic (which isn't a bad thing) or wants to become one, and in the shelter of your good company, I feel free to ask, "What is the human equivalent of antlers?" What do we humans have, whether it grows on our bodies or is a part of our collective culture—such as sports cars or neckties—that is comparable to antlers? I've been thinking about doing an online search for what Freudian theory might say . . . but I already know that the seemingly obvious answer of "phallic symbolism" isn't right. Fact is, a buck's antlers fall off every year and don't grow back for several months, and that's the end of *that* subject!

The next most obvious answer is that antlers are analogous to a king's crown, followed by weapons for battle. Hmmm! . . . A recent scientific strength analysis showed that deer antlers are sixteen times stronger than they have to be for display use, which rules out the crown. They *are* just the right strength for two bucks to lock antlers to safely test one another's overall physical abilities and level of determination. Whitetail and mule deer antlers appear to be designed to protect eyes and head during battle: a buck's antlers engage the other buck's for pushing, not stabbing. It's just guy stuff, like professional wrestling. (Moose, on the other hand, charge from a distance and slam right into each other with a loud but generally bloodless crash, sort of like a demolition derby with seat belts.) Therefore, antlers aren't exactly weapons—in fact, most deer species usually fight large predators with their front hooves, not their antlers . . . although an attacking coyote can expect to see a lowered set of sharp tines coming at him!

So, if antlers aren't represented in the human form as sex symbols, crowns, or weapons, what's left for us to consider? In Chapter 5, we'll see that there is a great physiological and nutritional cost required annually for a buck to grow its antlers, and I'm thinking now that antlers in the human form are, yes, the sports cars and other costly expressions of power and success, maybe even the benign but impressive appearance of a competitive body-builder. When Teddy Roosevelt, a "rugged individualist," ran for president on the Bull Moose Party ticket, the political cartoons of the day portrayed him wearing moose antlers.

In the twenty-first century, antlers are being used in advertising to sell everything from financial services to beer and propane gas. There's a mailbox down the road from my house that has deer antlers on it and

Theodore Roosevelt, candidate of the Bull Moose Party in 1912, was granted antlers by **Harper's Weekly** *for accepting corporate donations and his willingness to use military force where necessary to preserve peace.*

another one that supports a moose weathervane. A small company in Elk County, Pennsylvania, produces large, chocolate-covered elk-antler pretzels that have been shipped all over the country and even to Europe.

If anything, Europeans are more obsessed with antlers than we Americans are, and apparently they have been for nearly 40,000 years, since the Stone Age. We know this from the famous drawings on the walls of the Lascaux and Chauvet caves in southern France, which depict buck deer sporting huge antlers—no does, just bucks. Even now, most any pub in Germany or England will have a set of antlers on display against an impressive oak plaque; much of the time, they are just little spikes that we'd only make into knife handles.

VARIATIONS ON AN ANTLER THEME

All antlers are different. No two racks are alike—just like the people who are fascinated by them. I've asked dozens of people why they are so interested in antlers. "After all," I might say in order to keep the conversation going, "antlers are just bones." But once I have indicated with that comment that I might actually know something or other about antlers, they just seem inspired all the more to reveal the extent of their attraction to antlers, usually without giving me the explanation I'm seeking. These are people who are involved with antlers as shed-hunters, trophy hunters, taxidermists, artisan-carvers, and collectors, and in writing this book I had hoped to discover the universal answer to "What is the meaning of antlers?" Their first response often was mild irritation. They might say, "Why you asking *me*!?" as if any answer concerning antlers might reveal too much of their innermost thoughts. In the end, every one of them said enthusiastically, even passionately, that they had finally found something really worth being interested in, but none of them could provide the answer as to why.

Finally, I realized that it was because there is so much variation in antlers themselves. I don't mean just the physical structure—although that is a book in itself—but the ways in which antlers appeal to us and the ways we hope to use them for whatever personal gratification they might provide us. A big-game trophy-hunter who has successfully dropped whitetails, elk, caribou, and moose finally told me that antlers, being as different from one another as human fingerprints, provided the quarry with a specific identity, which let him focus on a certain buck or bull, thus making the hunt more challenging. One shed-hunter said that finding any antler, even one from a little spike buck, was a thrill because

Len Nagel, taxidermist and proprietor of the Antler Shed in West Valley, New York, adds a whitetail rack to an "antler tree."

it was once a part of a living animal. A successful businessman, who switched from restoring colonial New England homes to running an antler-supply business in Wyoming, still goes out to shed-hunt every chance he gets because, he says, it's the most satisfying work he's ever done. A professional carver, well known on eBay, claimed that he could "see" the dragons and eagles that were already contained within the curves and turns of an antler and he felt compelled to let them out. A Seneca-Onandaga Indian who I met at a pow-wow, and whose deceased father's antler artwork is displayed today in urban museums, told me that his people revered antlers (and the little figurines carved from them by his ancestors) as being spiritual in nature. And Dr. George Bubenik, mentioned several times elsewhere in this book, continues to contribute to international research into the medical mysteries of antlers, even as he enters retirement.

This is not just a male phenomenon, by the way. I know a woman taxidermist who has more mounted deer heads on the walls of her house, including the living room and even the kitchen, than I have ever seen in the woods during open season. She certainly seems to be a normal person, but one summer pastime that particularly delights both her and her patient husband is to set a full, four-legged mount of a buck with a big-antlered rack out on the lawn of their country home so that they can sit there on the porch and watch what people do as they drive by. Before long, though, they have to come back inside because their stomachs hurt so much from all the laughing.

Several of these antler fanatics are hunters or have hunted. But most are not regular deer hunters; many who classified themselves as such hadn't actually bought a license for several years. At any rate, most of the Antler People were into the antler game for other reasons than shooting a big buck. Being a hunter myself, this surprised me—really shocked me, in fact, when I first realized that antlers meant so many other things to other people. That's probably because, as a hunter, I felt that I had already experienced the "whole picture," in which I, the human predator, entered the wild world to hunt for meat—and if I got antlers with that meat, I got to keep those too. Now I value them in many different ways and at several levels, from aesthetic appeal to an appreciation of their natural history and science.

Antlers also can be worth a lot of money. Read on.

ANTLERS ARE WORTH A LOT OF BUCKS!

Nowhere is the strength of the antler market more apparent than the annual elk antler auction in Jackson Hole, Wyoming. Just imagine it: the entire town square and streets of Jackson Hole filled with four auctioneers, several sellers, around a hundred serious bidders, and about five *tons* of elk antlers for sale! Everyone there is involved in one way or

Jackson Hole, Wyoming, is the home of the largest annual elk antler auction. More than a thousand elk antlers are sold during one weekend each year.

another with the antler trade, including hundreds of Boy Scouts from the local district. In fact, the Boy Scouts are the ones who go into the wintering range of the elk in the National Elk Refuge and collect the antlers the elk have shed before their annual migration back to the summer range. A portion of the proceeds from the sale of the antlers goes to fund the winter elk-feeding program.

The average price per pound is market-driven and varies from year to year, from a high of $14 in recent years to a current average of about $10 per pound for "craft antlers," the ones that will be cut and machined into smaller parts for carving knife handles, buttons, belt buckles, and so on. Large, symmetrical antlers pull a considerably higher price and are usually bought by collectors and even interior decorators. In recent years, large chandeliers and furniture items assembled from elk antlers have become very popular, and antlers for this end use are often bundled together and sold as such.

There's a special excitement surrounding the event; people come from all over the United States, Canada, and occasionally parts of Asia. Around auction time, people run ads in the newspapers ("Antlers Wanted") and set up at intersections with signs ("We Buy Antlers" and "Will Work for Antlers"), and even the local recyclers and garbage collectors have gotten into the game.

For more information on the auction, go to www.jacksonholewy.net or www.jacksonholenet.com. The event is always scheduled for the third weekend in May.

As the Jackson Hole auction demonstrates, the antlers of the whitetail deer, mule deer, moose, and elk can fetch a high price these days. This might seem like the wrong thing to say, depending on who you're talking to, but it's true. Some folks might be concerned that the sport of deer hunting will suffer if we focus too much on money. But let's face it, we tend to take better care of whatever has value to us, and the problem of the imbalanced whitetail population—which can lead to damaged habitat and a reduction in antler sizes—is particularly in need of public attention.

There are three main markets for antlers: craft, fabrication, and trophy. These tend to overlap somewhat, especially where the paths of art and utilitarian function intersect, but this is the best way I can think of to give an overall picture of the antler trade. Keep in mind the fact that buying and selling of anything is a two-way street. If you're a carver and you personally find or otherwise acquire an antler, it's worth full value to you—the same amount that you would have had to pay to a dealer. But if you want to instead sell that same antler to a dealer, you'll get considerably less than full value.

Craft antlers are most often bought by people who are interested in machining, carving, and crafting them into a wide variety of objects, ranging from buttons and belt buckles to knife handles and fireplace tool holders . . . and on from there to beautifully carved works of art that can sell for thousands of dollars. In one form of the art, the palmated antler of the moose can be carved and cut all the way through, leaving a

Craft antlers come in many different sizes and shapes. The coronets shown here could be used for many articles, including medallions and decorative buttons, and the tines could be crafted into knife and fork handles. Nothing has to go to waste.

silhouetted wildlife scene or landscape. Antler bone is the "new ivory," replacing the elephant ivory that is no longer available to the independent artist except under special circumstances, and it also appeals to potential customers with its natural origins, especially when the annual shedding is explained to them.

Craft antlers are sold in all shapes and sizes, and in bits and pieces. On eBay, you could buy, for example, ten pounds of assorted antler tines. There are several small online companies that buy and sell antlers, whole and in pieces, including individual tines and coronets. Tines are often graded by quality, length, and whether they are curved or straight. If you want only a single elk antler tine, straight and about 9 inches long, to be made into a quirt-handle, for example, a typical price would be about $10 per piece, or roughly a dollar an inch. Thicker portions cut from the main beam of an elk antler are generally sold by weight, with prices ranging from $10 to $15 per pound. An artisan who's only interested in making knife handles obviously doesn't need a whole, perfect antler . . . and doesn't need to pay as much for his materials as does the

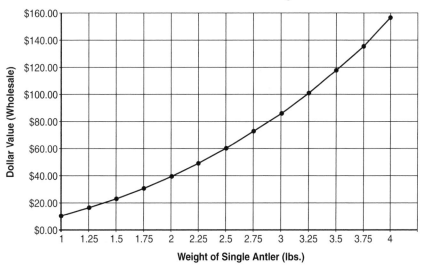

Whitetail Antler Dollar Value per Pound
for Antlercraft and Carving

artist who carves whole antlers into the shape of flying eagles or slithering dragons.

The prices of antlers vary from year to year, and from species to species. At one time within the past decade, elk antlers were selling for three times as much as whitetail and mule deer antlers, and then a few years later, after a prolonged winter cut the deer herds back in some western regions, the prices reversed themselves. Of course, the forces of supply and demand are always at work: as elk chandeliers continued to grow in popularity, the price for elk antlers climbed. But in a counter-current to that, as people saw these huge chandeliers in ski lodges and began looking for smaller deer-antler chandeliers for their own, smaller homes, deer antlers took off, too.

The graph above illustrates how antlers are priced; it is *not* intended to serve as an actual price chart. What I'm showing here is that the price per pound goes up at a greater rate for larger antlers. I've fixed the price at $10 for a single one-pound antler. Note that the price for a two-pound antler on this chart could be priced at $40 per pound, which would make the antler's value on this chart $80. And so on. For a visual perspective here, consider that a single antler from a modest six-point whitetail buck usually weighs only about one pound. As massiveness and the number of points increase, so does the price per pound, and when a deer's rack approaches a hypothetical Boone and Crockett Club score of about 150 inches, a single antler will usually weigh roughly three pounds. (Stay with me, please!) That single antler would be valued on this graph at $80 per pound, or $240. Both antlers together would cost $480. Now we're in trophy-price range, and if you look at the graph on page 32, you'll see that at around a score of 150, the criteria for dollar value shifts from simple weight to the intrinsic worth of pride of ownership.

Fabrication antlers are usually the larger shed antlers, and they're often sold tied together as kits or matched sets that are symmetrical and similar in color. They are used to build huge chandeliers, coffee table supports, lamps, and other fashionable items that can be found in private homes, restaurants, and ski lodges. Elk antlers are most popular here because of their large size and mass, but whitetail and mule deer antlers often fit together in more striking (although smaller) ways. Moose and caribou antlers are usually too big for this application.

Every day, thousands of antlers are available commercially. Tony Schaufler—co-owner, with his father Don, of the distribution company Antlers Unlimited (www.antlersunlimited.com)—routinely sorts through deep piles of antlers to identify, catalog, and appraise them for purchase or sale. Around 90 percent of the antlers shown here were naturally shed.

Many small businesses have developed to serve this market; consequently, the market has also grown for the amateur shed-hunter. Some of the major buyers of fabricated antler products are interior decorators, and their customers generally value class and style more than the money in their pocket. The market is especially good in the western U.S., where these items might sell for twice what they would in the East. Although the quality standards for fabrication antlers are higher than for craft antlers, it's often OK if there's a missing tine or a deformation, as long as the finished product can hide the flaw.

Trophy antlers are used entirely for display of one kind or another. The word "trophy" conjures up a vision of a personal prize, such as the spike buck antlers of a boy's first deer. Certainly the experienced big-game hunter too can be personally proud of a trophy rack obtained in a fair-chase hunt. But there also is a lively market for trophy antlers in which collectors, sportsmen, and interior decorators are involved. Trophy antlers are brought to this market in two different forms: either attached to the skull, as from a hunter's kill, and as loose shed antlers, in matched pairs.

Taxidermists occasionally buy trophy-class shed antlers to fill requests from customers who want mounted heads to display. Remember, because buck deer lose their antlers every year, there are potentially many more shed antlers to be found than bucks. In order to mount shed antlers on a deer head, the taxidermist has to estimate what the original inside-spread measurement was, and then affix the antlers accordingly to a mounting form. (The taxidermist will need to acquire a deer skin to finish the mount, but that's a different subject.) Even replica antlers, which are usually molded copies of famous trophy racks, are valued from several hundred to a few thousand dollars.

The main standard by which trophy antlers are judged and valued is the Boone and Crockett score. (See Chapter 4 for more details on scoring.) Individual collectors may have a particular liking for unusual antlers, such as those having drop-tines or other uncommon characteristics, and they will often pay more than the Boone and Crockett score might seem to warrant. Recently, the King Ranch in Texas began charging their successful deer-hunting clients a price per inch for trophy antlers. For a Boone and Crockett gross score of 150 inches (which is too low to be entered in the record books), the price is $36.66 per inch, for a total of $5,500. For a buck in the 200-inch range, the price is an even $100 per inch, or $20,000.

The graph on the next page plots the estimated approximate values for "typical" trophy antlers in 1994 and 2004, relative to Boone and

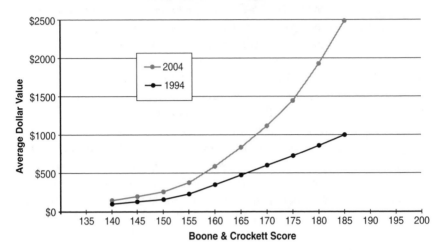

Whitetail Antler Dollar Values vs. Boone & Crockett Scores

Crockett scores. In this context, the word "trophy" means that the antlers must still be attached to the skull of a deer that was taken in "fair chase," as defined by the Boone and Crockett Club. While it's true that a deer mounted with shed antlers (and the hide of some other deer) can certainly *look* like a trophy, the critical measurement of the inside spread would always be unknown. The "fair chase" requirement excludes deer killed within a high-fence preserve, game farm, or zoo. However, road-kills, deer that are found dead in the wild, and even old mounts found in someone's attic are accepted and classified as "picked-up" or "found." In fact, the current top two non-typical whitetails are in this category.

There are three trends revealed here. The first is obvious and expected, which is the greater value placed on higher B&C scores. Bigger antlers sell at a higher price than do smaller ones—no surprise there! The second trend is that trophy antlers were worth more in 2004 than in 1994, by a margin much greater than could be explained by simple inflation. But notice how over the ten-year period the price for the highest-scoring antlers increased more than the price for lower-scoring antlers. Moving from left to right across the graph, a significant difference in valuation between 1994 and 2004 begins around the B&C score of 160, which is the entry level for "typical" whitetail antlers. From this point on, the higher scores all highlight the fact that these are officially trophies. Bragging rights belong to anyone who possesses a

Trophy antlers are impressive . . . and impressively expensive.
These antlers hold the world record for a non-typical mule
deer; they were recently purchased by Don Schaufler for a
reported $225,000 from the Broder family in Saskatchewan.

160-plus whitetail rack. At a score of 170, the antlers would have sold for a ballpark price of $600 in 1994, and $1,120 in 2004—a little less than two times as much. Looking at the 185 score, the difference is even greater: $1,000 in 1994 compared to $2,500 in 2004, or two-and-a-half times as much.

Where the money really starts to fall like the leaves off a maple tree in late October is when the Boone and Crockett score for typical whitetails goes to 190 inches and above. Now we're talking real money. This is lift-off time, but I couldn't show it on the graph because this book's page wasn't big enough! Since the year 1900, there have been only 128 typical whitetail bucks listed in the Boone and Crockett database that have scored 190 or above. Consequently, their racks are each worth a small fortune by normal standards. Of these 128 sets of trophy antlers, twenty-two (17.2 percent) are now owned by Bass Pro Shops, which recently bought Larry Huffman's world-famous collection of trophy whitetail antlers. Cabela's has also been a player in the whitetail market, but they currently own only three of the top 190-scored typical whitetail antlers, and they are apparently targeting the mule deer antler market instead. Cabela's owns eleven (22.0 percent) of the top fifty typical mule deer antlers, including the Number 1 "Doug Burris Jr." mule deer taken in Dolores, Colorado, in 1972 that scored 226 $^4/_8$ inches.

WHO'S BUYING ALL THE B&C TROPHY ANTLERS?

CATEGORY	CABELA'S, INC.	BASS PRO SHOPS
Whitetail (typical)	24	36
Whitetail (non-typical)	10	81
Mule Deer (typical)	29	1
Mule Deer (non-typical)	96	0
Elk (typical)	8	0
Elk (non-typical)	9	1
Caribou	4	2
Moose	0	0
TOTALS	180	121

Overall, the market value of trophy antlers is influenced by these two retailers in ways that aren't immediately apparent. On one hand, it would seem that their involvement in the trophy antler market would push prices up, since there are only so many top-score antlers to go around, and the overall demand is high. For example, only five typical whitetails over 190 were registered in 2003. Compare this to the 267 bucks registered during that same time that scored higher than the 160 entry-level mark, all of them potential collectors' items. In some ways, Cabela's and Bass Pro Shops often define what the prices should be for the high-end trophies, since the competition is marginalized. Still, the individual hunter is in no rush to sell his lifetime trophy unless the offered price is just right.

The table above shows that an astonishing total of over three hundred sets of Boone and Crockett Club antlers are now owned by only two buyers. Prices rise when two or more parties compete with one another. But Cabela's tends to specialize in mule deer antlers while Bass Pro focuses even more sharply on whitetail antlers, which tempers the potentially inflationary effect they could have on trophy prices.

There's another interesting trend, which is that both companies are putting their money on non-typical antlers far more often than on typical antlers, each in their own chosen market. Elsewhere in this book, we'll see that non-typical antlers occur in only one-quarter to one-third of bucks registered with Boone and Crockett, but Cabela's is buying these non-typicals 64 percent of the time and Bass Pro is 68 percent of the time. Non-typical antlers definitely have more shock appeal and are probably more effective in attracting potential customers into stores, which in itself is an "antler quality factor" (like points and spreads) that hasn't ever been "scored" before in terms of dollar value. Both Cabela's and Bass Pro Shops have also been buying smaller whitetail and mule deer antlers and a very few of elk and caribou as well. Why are they doing this? Well . . . I couldn't get a direct answer to this question from either company, but it's a pretty good guess that having a variety of trophy antlers on display pulls people into stores.

What all this means is that people are more interested in collecting trophy antlers now than probably ever before. There also are more people participating in the antler market today, both buyers and sellers. What many years ago used to be a tight little circle of wealthy buyers and fast-talking brokers, some of them trying to outsmart the others and many of them competing to see who could dupe the innocent rural deer hunter into giving up his trophy for peanuts, has ended. The Internet has become the great equalizer of the antler market. Now we're all in the act!

HOW THE INTERNET BROUGHT ALL
OF US ANTLER PEOPLE TOGETHER

When the Internet and e-mail first became available to the average person in the early 1990s, to the extent that ordinary folks began taking it seriously—as something more than just a better way to do genealogies and find a recipe for chocolate-chip cookies—many sociologists began predicting an end to worldwide cultural diversity. They prophesized that the whole world would soon morph into bland oneness, with everyone using the same cookie recipe, as it were.

Instead, just the opposite happened. The increased communication led to a flourishing of specialized interests. The Albanians began finding each other and setting up Albanian websites, just as the Zambians did, and all the rest of us in between, and within a few years, there were found to be more ways to bake chocolate-chip cookies than had ever existed. "Affinity groups" formed online and among them, we Antler People found each other.

In the early 1990s, most antlers-for-sale were advertised mainly by word of mouth and in the classified ads of taxidermy and trapper magazines. Even though eBay started up in 1995, it wasn't until about 1999 that it became a significant influence in the antler market, and at that early date, there were only about fifty different sets of antler materials being auctioned daily, by even fewer sellers. Within five years, however,

Shown here are shed whitetail antlers in the display room of taxidermist and whitetail specialist Bill Yox.

the number of antler items being auctioned at any given moment was around a thousand. Today, most of these items are for craft antlers for carvers and artisans, but there sometimes are impressive racks for collectors . . . often at impressive prices!

OWNERSHIP: PRIDE AND PREJUDICE

There's still a lingering prejudice against owning and displaying antlers that you didn't personally find as springtime sheds or remove from a deer that you killed during open season. Generally this attitude is expressed by people who haven't yet learned what the new antler phenomenon is all about. They hold the opinion that anyone who has a set of antlers over their fireplace is either a successful hunter or an insecure fraud. They just don't "get it."

All this is changing, however, especially in the world of the collector, but also in the workshops of the carvers and artisans. The word "trophy" in the context of big antlers also is falling out of favor because, like a bowling trophy, it connotes a singular achievement or a one-time event. Now, antlers are being appreciated by more and more people in a variety of ways. They're now seen not just as bones scavenged from a deer, but as fascinating natural sculptures that can tug at the Paleolithic part of our souls—the part that still responds to antlers in their many forms and functions.

3

SHED-HUNTING: "LOST AND FOUND" IN THE WOODS

WHAT'S IT ALL ABOUT?

Shed antlers are a renewable resource. Buck deer lose their antlers every year, usually late in the winter; the specific time depends on the weather, altitude, snow cover, and food supply. Soon after the antlers drop, shed-hunters begin venturing into the woods to find them. Shed-hunting has emerged over the last ten years or so as one of the very best ways to excuse yourself from having to help with spring cleaning, and it has recently become especially popular. It's a sport that the entire family can enjoy, and it's a great way to get your partner and the kids more interested in the outdoors and to help them learn how to really *see* nature. You'll sharpen your own eye as well. There's a certain excitement to knowing that the buck whose antlers you've just found is probably still very much alive (most deer hunting seasons end before bucks begin to shed) and might already have begun growing another set.

The outdoorsmen who first popularized shed-hunting weren't looking for antlers; they were in the woods seeking the signs and sounds of spring gobbler turkeys. Over the last couple of decades, the population of wild turkeys—and the popularity of hunting them—grew at an enormous rate, and the result was many more thousands of hunters in the springtime woodlands. The deer population also increased greatly, which resulted in more antlers being shed, and the net effect was more people finding more antlers. Pretty soon, shed antlers were showing up all over the place wherever braggarts gathered. Turkey hunters began boasting about the antlers they'd found more than the weights of the gobblers they had bagged. They could have kept their mouths shut and kept this sport all to themselves, but that's asking an awful lot of the typical spring turkey hunter.

As we've seen, though, a lot of the people who collect antlers or utilize them in carving or fabrication aren't hunters and have no interest in ever being one. One fellow I met on eBay told me that he'd stopped being a regular hunter and had become a shed-hunter because that way he didn't have to kill anything to get the antlers, and sheds were a lot easier to haul out of the woods.

Most of the shed-hunters I've spoken to seem to have gone a bit bonkers about the sport. Actually . . . yeah, they all have. One experienced fellow told me that the first time he purposely went out shed-hunting, he didn't find a thing and began to think that he was wasting his time. The next day, in a different part of the same woods, he found his first shed antler and instantly became addicted. Another fellow affectionately says, "It's all about boneheads looking for head bones." The discovery of even a single little spike antler is a treasured event, because shed-hunting is about more than just "finding something"—instead, it almost feels like a personal contact with the deer. These days, shed-hunting has become so popular that several outfitters now offer planned shed-hunts for up to $200 a day.

WHERE TO FIND SHED ANTLERS

How difficult is it to find a shed antler? Let's do the numbers and put this question in perspective. In whitetail deer country, which these days is just about everywhere except in your house and maybe up on the roof (except on Christmas Eve . . . no, wait—those are caribou), the approximate average post-hunt population density could be about thirty deer per square mile. Of those deer, probably only five are bucks with antlers. (That's because each year approximately 60 to 75 percent of all bucks are killed each season.) These bucks each have two antlers, so when they're shed, that's ten shed antlers per square mile. If you didn't know anything about the movements of deer, you'd have to search sixty-four acres (one-tenth of a square mile) to maybe find one antler. That's an area approximately equal to five football fields side-by-side, including the goalposts, the benches, and the cheerleaders.

One antler . . . or you could search all day and not even find one. Here's where the experienced deer hunter has an advantage. You look for shed antlers where you'd hunt for deer. Taking this a step further, the odds are good that wherever you find shed antlers this spring, you'll find the bucks that grew them next fall. Consider this: if during the fall hunting season you find a large deer track in the snow or soft ground, the only thing you positively know about that mystery deer is that it has big feet. (Either that, or you're in a cow pasture.) But when

Late winter is a good time to hunt for antler sheds in the northern states: the snow has mostly melted and the weeds are still flattened. Here a whitetail antler has been found by Doug Coleman (dtcoleman@cableone.net), producer of the videotape "Through the Eyes of a Shed Hunter."

you find an antler, you know for certain that a buck has been there. Obviously, this works the other way around, too; if you look where you saw bucks last autumn, you're more apt to find their shed antlers later, in the spring.

The successful shed-hunter has learned not just where to look, but *how* to look—how to scan the ground without losing his sense of direction. Those of us who are deer hunters are self-trained to look for game at the extreme range of our line of sight most of the time, and only occasionally to look down at where our feet are for tracks and other signs of deer. The shed-hunter needs to look somewhere in between the far and the near in order to discover antler tips projecting above receding snow . . . or the bent, brown beam of an antler among the straight, gray trunks of fallen branches and snow-twisted vines.

Develop a strategy for finding shed antlers the same way you would find deer. During the summer, both the bucks and the does tend to use the same routes between bedding areas and feeding areas almost every day. But once the rut (the breeding season) begins in the fall, bucks change those travel patterns so as to keep track of female deer by means of scent, whether or not the does are yet in heat. Following well-established deer trails through the woods is better than nothing, but bucks during the rut are inclined just to intercept these trails, not walk along them. They are more often seen traveling along or just inside the contours of heavy cover, such as dense thickets, or along the edges of agricultural fields, hedgerows, and wooded drainage ditches.

Bedding areas are excellent places to look for shed antlers because the bucks spend a lot of time during the day resting in one place, and their antlers are just as apt to shed there as elsewhere. The actual shedding of antlers occurs in late winter, a time of year when deer are more apt to bed down on the southeastern sides of slopes that see more of the sun and provide some protection from those cold winter winds. Big bucks usually squeeze into the heaviest cover they can find, and that's where you need to put your head down and push your way through. Once you're in there, look for deer trails and also for rubs where deer have scraped the bark off saplings while removing their autumn velvet.

Shed-hunters have told me they've more than once found two shed antlers lying perfectly side by side, as though the deer had sneezed and blown them off. Sheds are often found next to where the buck has bedded down for the night, which makes sense since in late winter or spring, deer usually spend a lot of their time either resting or eating. (Can you imagine how it would feel to wake up in the morning without your antlers?) Deer tend not to travel much in bad winter weather, and if the snow has been deep and the deer have "yarded up," you'll probably be able to find more matched pairs in the general area around its bed. (It's important that you don't put any extra stress on the yarded deer with your late-winter shed-hunting, so stay out of the bedding area itself, at least until the snow cover has melted to a shallow depth.) Finding a matched pair is usually a rare event, and most of the time, even if you do eventually find the second antler, it will have fallen a lot farther away than you had hoped.

Although in an emergency a deer can plunge into or jump over the kind of impenetrable cover that even a small dog would have difficulty getting through, some of the time they take the easy way . . . just like you would. Such shortcuts often include hayfields along well-established trails, which aren't hard to find in the tall grasses once you know what to look for, and which generally remain the same from year to year. My personal experience with deer trails is this: whenever I'm casually walking through the woods where I live—in western New York State, just four miles north of the Pennsylvania border—if I look down, I can usually find a deer print close by. This often means that I've been following a deer trail unintentionally, just because it was the easiest path for me to follow.

Open fields in snow country can be great places to look for antlers if the snow was shallow at the time of year that bucks were dropping their antlers. For example, shedding reaches a peak around the middle of February where I live. If the snow is shallow then, deer move out into the fields at night to paw the ground for the underlying green herbs and weeds. But if the snow is too deep, they

A deer bed in the snow, recently vacated except for the shed antler that the buck left behind.

remain back in the woods in search of other foods and shed their antlers there. One local shed-hunter told me that if the right combination of winter snow and the peak of shedding occur, it's possible to find maybe even a dozen antlers within a few acres of open field once the snow thaws.

Shed antlers so commonly appear along trails through hayfields and other agricultural fields that they're found too often (and too late!) stuck into the tires of farmers' tractors, causing expensive flats. It's a common event. Think about the odds: the tread of a farm tractor covers maybe 20 percent of the width of the tractor's path, which means that every five times a farmer tills a field or cuts hay where there's a fallen antler, he will either squash the antler into the earth or suffer a punctured tire. I personally know of two men who have had antler-flattened tires just within the past year.

SHED ANTLERS BY AGE OF WHITETAIL BUCKS

The odds are that nearly two out of three shed antlers you find will be little spikes or fork horns from yearling bucks. Well, maybe not—big antlers are easier to find than small ones. But if you want to know the probable breakdown of antlers by age out there on the forest floor, take a look at the following table.

AGE DISTRIBUTION OF SHED ANTLERS

AGE (YEARS)	PERCENTAGE OF ANTLERED BUCKS
1 1/2	60
2 1/2	24
3 1/2	10
4 1/2	6

This age structure results from a consistent mortality rate of 60 percent during the hunting season that's spread equally across all age groups. The "Percentage of Antlered Bucks" numbers will be the same both before and after the hunting season. The difference is that there will be only 40 percent as many bucks left to shed their antlers after the hunting season. The other antlers were taken home by lucky hunters.

WHAT TO LOOK FOR IN A SHED ANTLER

Antlers are shed following the rut, when the buck's testosterone drops below a level that is needed for the continued sustenance of living bone. This complex process is controlled in part by declining sunlight and usually happens in a surprisingly short time, sometimes just a few days or less. The seal connecting the antler to the pedicle begins to weaken, and whereas one day a buck could be dragged from the woods by his antlers, they might fall off easily a day or two later if he moves his head too quickly. Usually, only one antler falls off first, followed soon—but maybe not until five miles later—by the other one. Whitetail bucks often shake their heads vigorously to rid themselves of the imbalance of only one antler. Gary Alt, a Pennsylvania wildlife biologist, reports having seen a captive buck that, having just lost one antler, wedged the remaining antler in the fork of a tree and wrenched it off—including with it, unfortunately, a bloody piece of its skull. The buck survived, but the next two years the antler that grew there was misshapen.

The seal of an antler can be a useful indicator of the relative health and testosterone level of the buck that shed it. Look at the base of the antler where it had been attached to the buck's skull. If it bulges outwardly, the buck's virility and health are proportionate to the size of the bulge—the more, the better.

If the seal is concave (shown as a negative value on the graph on the next page), this indicates that the buck was (and probably still is) nutritionally deprived, had an abnormally low level of testosterone in its blood, or was an older buck in the decline of its life. Or, perhaps, all

Whitetail Buck Testosterone Levels vs. Depth of Antler Seal after Shedding

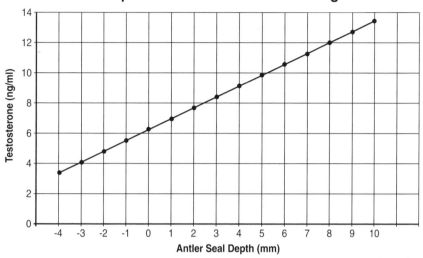

three. The graph compares the seal depth in millimeters to the testosterone level. (One millimeter converts to just a hair more than $^1/_{32}$ inch.) This relationship is based on research on the whitetail deer in North America by Dr. George Bubenik. Seal depth is routinely used in Europe by wildlife managers to evaluate the ongoing health of the local deer herd (usually red deer and fallow deer), but its use hasn't been standardized in America, where studies of deer sex and age ratios have gained the higher ground. But for the dedicated

The shape of the seal on the butt-end of a shed antler is an indicator of the buck's testosterone level and overall health.

whitetail shed-hunter who might have been following and collecting the antlers of the same big buck for a number of years, the annual trend in that deer's seal depth can be far more interesting than any summer's golf average.

VALUES OF SHED ANTLERS

The worth of a shed antler depends on several factors. Of course, the value is greatest to the person who found it, and many if not most shed-hunters won't even consider selling their treasured antlers. As with any "trophy" sport, shed-hunters tend to remember every find—where the antler was first seen, and how it felt to pick it up and brush off the leaves and mud. Still, it's nice to know just as a matter of personal interest what an antler might be worth if you wanted to auction it online or sell it to the craft or collectors' markets.

The most valuable antlers are ranked as "Number 1 Browns." They are freshly dropped and free of flaws such as broken tines. There are several possible markets for these, including craft, fabrication, and trophy display, depending on the size and quality. Craft antlers of small size are worth around $10 per pound, but as we've seen, the price per pound increases as the antler size goes up. Shed antlers with reasonably high Boone and Crockett scores might be worth several hundred dollars, and possibly even several thousand if you find the matching antler! However, the market prices can be highly variable from year to year.

Antler flaws can fall into several categories, listed here in order of increasing seriousness:

Bleached antlers have been exposed to the sun too long. A bleached antler can be restored to a more natural color with a thin solution of wood stain, but it would be unethical to sell it as a "brown" antler.

Chalky antlers have been exposed for a year or more to the combined effects of rain, sunlight, and cyclical temperature changes. They become porous near the surface due to oxidation and the leaching of calcium. Some value as a carving material has been lost.

Cracked antlers are judged on the extent of the cracking, since an artist-carver or artisan can usually get some good out of the rest of the antler. If the antler was cracked while it was still in velvet and then grew in non-typical ways, it could actually be worth more.

Chewed antlers are the least valuable per pound because they're usually badly disfigured from the gnawing of porcupines and red and gray squirrels, who chew for the calcium, phosphorous, and other minerals that antlers contain. Antlers that are shed in an oak forest inhabited by squirrels will literally be chewed to pieces as rapidly as the melting snow exposes them. Mice also will occasionally nibble on an antler, but antlers found in open fields, where mice are most common and the other critters seldom venture, are often completely free of chew-

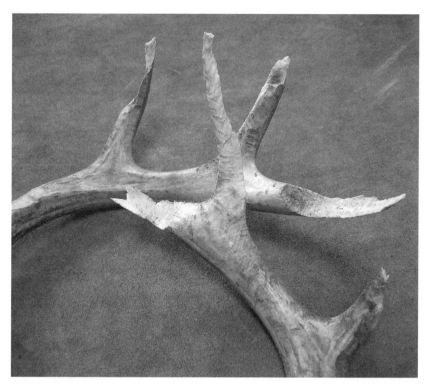

Shed antlers are often destroyed by rodents both large and small.

ing. Still, if you found a chewed antler that was worthy of record-book status based on size and points, you'd definitely have a prize worth more than just a few dollars a pound.

An important personal achievement in shed-hunting is finding the second antler of the same buck. Match-ups might be questioned by other collectors, but you know you've got one when you find the second antler lying there on the ground! Deer antlers from two bucks can look a lot alike, but a match-up is hard to deny. The structure and design of antlers are genetically determined, the way fingerprints are in humans. Once you've found both antlers, you have a pair that can be mounted and even unofficially scored using Boone and Crockett methods, if you estimate the inside spread. What comes next? Well, you follow that buck for your next prize, which is finding both of its antlers the following year. And the year after. Shed-hunting is one sport where the game never ends.

Possession and selling or buying of any part of a legal game animal is regulated to one extent or another in most if not all states. This generally hasn't been a big deal as far as the antler trade is concerned, but your best bet would be to contact your state's Department of Natural Resources. In California, where eBay is headquartered and therefore subject to that state's laws, the Fish and Game Code authorizes the sale of shed antlers (including the antlers of farmed deer) that have been manufactured into saleable items or cut into blocks for further modification. In New York State, the laws that I've been able to find are generally quite liberal for the handling of shed antlers, skulls, or antler pieces for use in arts and crafts and on mounted taxidermy specimens such as you might find for sale. But, during the actual deer hunting season, I'm thinking that if I had a set of antlers attached to a freshly cut buck skull with flecks of raw flesh still attached, I'd want very much to have either a hunting tag attached to it or a very plausible story to tell if someone in a dark green uniform was asking me questions.

DOGS FOR SHED-HUNTING

Almost any dog that stays close to you in the woods can be trained to help you find shed antlers. Labradors and the other retrieving breeds are naturally good at hunting for antlers because of their innate desire to please and their instincts for finding things on the ground by sight as well as scent. The so-called versatile breeds, especially the German Shorthair Pointer, are also well-suited for seeking antlers because of their inclination to "hunt dead"—to eagerly retrieve killed game— whether it's feathered or furred. Beagles and other hounds also have the enthusiasm and scenting ability to find antlers, but not the same willingness to share—that is, to let you know what they've found. Pointers and Setters are bred to generally take their scent from the air, not off the ground, so they are usually not at their best looking for antlers. Still, any dog that will listen to you even just some of the time can be trained to eagerly search for shed antlers. Most dogs, regardless of breed or lack of breeding, are inclined to eventually do what you want them to do . . . except to stay off the couch when you leave the room.

As humans, we might think that, to a dog, an antler would only smell like an ordinary deer bone (which it is), but some good shed-hunting dogs can even locate an antler hidden under snow. That's actually not a big deal: my beagles can follow a rabbit trail across an icy pond in freezing temperatures when the wind is howling. Dogs are known to have an ability to detect scent somewhere between ten thousand and a hundred thousand times greater than ours. A serious shed-hunter can rather easily teach his dog how to apply that phenomenal ability to finding antlers. Antlers definitely have an odor while still in velvet, and it's now understood that their scent glands serve to broadcast certain pheromones as the rut approaches. As mentioned earlier, the velvet skin contains the highest concentration of oil-producing glands of any other place on the deer's hide. Most of this scent is, of course, lost as the velvet is rubbed off, but bucks continue to add new scent by rubbing the glands just below their eyes and then their hard antlers against branches. Bucks also try to get their urine spread onto their hardened antlers . . . never mind how. Apparently, a little goes a long way. Still, by the time a shed antler has lain on the ground for a few months, it has been soaked with a variety of other scents as well.

Training a dog to find shed antlers isn't difficult, but the dog needs to be taught that antlers are the name of the game, not live deer, or rabbits, or mice. Doug and Tammy Coleman, shed-hunters from Lewiston, Idaho, have produced a shed-hunting video that shows their black Labrador, "Cowboy," in action during some of the scenes. I asked Tammy how she trained him for shed-hunting. She said that the first step was to teach the dog, as a puppy, to expect a reward for such basic

"Cowboy," a Labrador belonging to Doug and Tammy Coleman, with the NASHC record-book whitetail sheds that he found in Saskatchewan in 2004.

commands as sit, stay, and fetch. In the early stages of any dog-training program, it's vitally important to reward a dog as quickly as possible, even to the extent of placing the tidbit directly in his mouth rather than waiting for him to request it. Tammy used ordinary dry doggy bones, but some dogs have more discerning personal tastes and prefer jerky or something with more flavor. The idea here was to create a communication link for teaching the dog the more difficult tasks later.

She then got Cowboy involved in retrieving a rubber ball, then some other objects, and finally a small antler—at which point she began rewarding the dog only for retrieving the antler. Cowboy caught on to that very quickly, learning not to bother with the other stuff. The next step involved throwing the antler with the dog watching, but in such a way that Cowboy couldn't see where it landed and would have to search for it while being told, "Find it!" Then, in a nearby wooded area, Tammy would routinely hide several antlers and tell the dog to find them, waiting until all had been found and retrieved.

Later, on real shed-hunting ventures, Tammy learned that she had to have the treat immediately ready for the dog; otherwise, he'd stop several yards away and drop the antler. If Tammy happens to see a shed before the dog does, she stays away from it and uses the find command to reinforce what she wants the dog to understand. She also points toward the shed to teach the dog to look to her for hand signals. Labs are routinely taught to obey hand signals as part of a "fetching" program; they almost seem to have an inborn instinct to do so. The hound breeds are typically the least able to respond to hand signals, but most other dog breeds catch on to this tactic fairly easily. The trick is to get the dog to believe that you know where an antler is when he doesn't. By incorporating hand signals early in the training program, as with the "hidden antler" game that Tammy played with Cowboy, you'll soon teach a dog to look to you for guidance, especially if a reward is involved.

An eager dog can also be taught to move back and forth like a windshield-wiper. When both Tammy and Doug are walking through the same general area, Cowboy will often range between them, which provides him with more ground to cover. In addition to hand signals, one way to get a dog to range from side to side is to keep changing your own direction as you walk through the woods and fields. A young dog has an instinctual fear of being abandoned, and it will keep looking back to check on you to make sure that he's headed where you are going. This is also a good way to teach a young dog the "Come!" command, which comes in mighty handy when he later strays out of sight.

If you haven't already yard-trained the young dog to come when called, you can easily do it in the woods just by turning around and walking directly away, calling out the command one time. (I said *one* time! If you call four times for a dog to come, then you're teaching him to come only if you say it four times.) When you see the dog coming, continue going away until he is right beside you, and then reward him with sweet talk and a treat.

Cowboy has learned to find and follow deer trails and now also does his fair share of brush-busting when instructed to do so. Sometimes, when scenting conditions are poor, the dog will appear to have lost interest or be having an off day. But, Tammy said, there have been several times that's happened, and a serious shed-hunt has turned into just a walk in the woods, when all of a sudden Cowboy will appear unexpectedly beside her with an antler in his mouth.

A dog new to shed-hunting might, at first exposure in the woods, be more interested in tracking live deer and even in chasing them. Besides being illegal in most states, harassing deer in late winter (especially if they're yarded up) and early spring stresses them and needs to be stopped before it begins. You have to walk a fine line to solve this

Tammy Coleman and Cowboy with their newfound sheds and a fork-horn's skull. The Lab was trained by Tammy using the methods described in this chapter.

problem, because punishing a dog for showing an interest in deer could inadvertently turn him off on antlers. Still, a shed antler is a dry bone that smells like one and lies very still on the ground, and a live deer is a big, strongly scented, hairy animal that runs away. If you continue your training program to reinforce and even enhance the dog's eagerness to find shed antlers, you can usually solve the live deer problem by treating it as a separate problem with conventional methods.

Once you've found a deer's shed antler, finding the second antler then becomes the real challenge, and here is where a dog can really shine. There's no scientific data that I could find that documents the average distance on the ground between the loss of the first and second antlers. It's fairly well known that a buck might carry the single remaining antler for several days, dropping it miles away from the first. As mentioned earlier, some shed-hunters have found both antlers side by side or even in a pile, sometimes beside where a deer has bedded for the day. But, finding the second antler is seldom that easy. You look . . . and you look . . . but you still don't find it. Having a dog along, one that you've successfully trained to shed-hunt, can be very reassuring under these circumstances. I'll never be able to prove this, but I think that most dogs are so acutely sensitive to smell that a shed-hunting dog with a good nose and a desire to please you could eventually teach itself to actually follow the buck's trail just for the purpose of finding the second antler.

Son Mike Coleman with an elk shed antler.

THE NORTH AMERICAN SHED HUNTERS CLUB

The NASHC (www.shedantlers.org) serves as the official record-keeping organization for all North American shed antler scores. The club was established in 1991 in Minnesota and then moved to Lyndon Station, Wisconsin, in 2002. The *North American Shed Hunter* newsletter is published quarterly and sent to all members and certified scorers. I've been very impressed by what this not-for-profit organization is doing to get everybody off of the couch and into the woods by promoting shed-hunting as a family sport. The NASHC is authorized by the Boone and Crockett Club to apply their scoring techniques to single antlers, the scores of which can then be entered into the NASHC record book. There are 140 official scorers in thirty-four states available to members for certification of their shed scores.

The organization also has a record-book category for shed antlers found in "high fence" areas such as zoos, game farms, and fenced-in hunting preserves. The Boone and Crockett Club, on the other hand, accepts only the antlers of "wild" deer species killed in fair chase, in accidents (such as being hit by a car), or by natural causes, and that is as it should be. But for shed scoring, no deer needs to be killed to produce an antler that qualifies for the NASHC record books, and there's much genuine interest in what the "high fence" deer are capable of producing under controlled genetic and environmental conditions.

For details on scoring single sheds, see page 70.

4

KEEPING SCORE: HOW TO MEASURE ANTLERS

WHY KEEP SCORE?

A common fallacy is that only the big-game trophy hunters are interested in what the numerical score of a set of antlers might be. That's particularly ironic, because the purpose of the original scientific and biological organizations that were the forerunners of the Boone and Crockett Club was simply to document, as well as could be done, the measurements of deer, elk, moose, and caribou antlers before these and other big game animals were driven into extinction. Yes, a hundred years ago, the eastern United States was nearly devoid of big game animals, and just about everyone in a position to know about such things had decided that the final push of civilization from the Mississippi to the West Coast would result in their extinction.

The Boone and Crockett Club was founded in 1887 by Theodore Roosevelt to establish a coalition of conservationists and hunters who would begin to address the issues that were then affecting wildlife and wild habitat. In conjunction with the Bronx Zoo, naturalists and scientists of the Boone and Crockett Club set out to collect and measure all the trophy-size heads that they could find in private collections so that a final record could be made of the grandeur that existed and was expected to disappear. But, how to measure what had been and what could yet be? Other than habitat and population studies, the only other manageable way was to monitor the sizes of antlers that were annually produced by deer, elk, moose, and caribou. By 1950, the Boone and Crockett scoring system, in which the lengths and circumferences of antlers are carefully measured, had become universally accepted.

For most North American deer species, the long-term result of this attention has been an outstanding success story in modern game man-

In this early Boone and Crockett Club photograph, the main beam circumference of the A. S. Reed Alaska-Yukon moose is measured by Grancel Fritz, who helped establish the scoring system still in use today. This moose was killed in 1900, scored 240 7/8 inches, and over a century later is still ranked Number 49.

agement. Today, the Boone and Crockett antler measurement data are used for a variety of game management projects, particularly because a buck's antlers develop in direct response to the habitat in which he lives, and (this is particularly important) the age to which he survives. Thicker, longer, and broader antlers indicate not only good habitat but also suggest a more balanced male/female ratio, for reasons we'll go into in Chapter 10.

But the point here for antler fanatics like you and me is that Boone and Crockett Club scores provide us with a universally accepted measure of economic and aesthetic value, whether we be hunters, collectors, carvers, fabricators, or, um, just plain nuts about antlers with no other rationalization needed. Knowing this, can you even begin to consider buying or selling any antlers without knowing their score?

DOES KEEPING SCORE INTERFERE WITH
THE SPORTING ETHIC OF HUNTING?

Well . . . no, I don't think so, at least when it comes down to scoring antlers. Consider this story: A couple of decades ago I shot a nine-point whitetail buck in the woods behind my house that was a trophy in the finest sense of the word. Three inches of snow had fallen by sunup, and it was still falling late in the morning when I found the tracks of this deer. I had been still-hunting and a steady wind was blowing just hard enough to cover the sound of my footsteps—and it was blowing toward me, not the deer. I didn't know whether I was tracking a doe or a buck, but I didn't much care; at that point in my life I hadn't yet caught the antler virus and was more interested in venison.

After two miles of very slow tracking, I realized that the deer knew I was in the woods by the way it would hook to one side or another to look back in my direction. The hunt became a game of chess, of who had the best position. I decided that the odds were good that the deer would bed down atop a little rise in an otherwise boggy area of the woods. From there, it would be able to keep a watch in my direction and smell approaching danger from the other direction. My only chance at getting a responsible shot at the deer would be by coming in from the side, so I walked straight away from the deer's trail and made a wide sweep of about a quarter mile to a position maybe fifty yards past where I had bet the deer would have bedded down. I stayed out of the windstream until it died down momentarily, and then I walked quickly but quietly toward the clearing above where I thought the deer would be. Then, as planned, I suddenly stopped—I absolutely froze in place with the gun pointed ahead and began studying every shadow, every twig that probed above the snow in the dense brush. Nothing. I waited, and waited some more . . . the wind picked up a bit . . . and then two of those twigs grew taller and turned, and I saw deer ears, then eyes, and I killed the buck right there on its bed. That was my trophy: not the nine points nor the buck itself, but the achievement of having stalked a deer to within twenty yards of its concealment. I saw it before it saw me.

Yes, the buck was a nine-point, as are about 15 percent of the several thousand trophy typical whitetails scored and registered by the Boone and Crockett Club. But my particular nine-point wasn't anywhere near that exalted status. In fact, and I'm a bit embarrassed to tell you this, the inside spread between the antlers of my still-hunted, killed-on-its-bed "trophy" buck was only about 10 inches. (Most B&C whitetails have spreads well over 20 inches; the widest on record is over 34 inches.)

It gets even worse. My humble buck actually won a local deer contest. A country neighbor of mine, George, was hosting a contest that year for a couple dozen of us hunters. There were two rules: it couldn't be a roadkill, and George had to be shown the buck so he could count the points. Some folks have the mistaken impression that the number of points on a deer's rack is an indicator of its age in years, and therefore its impressiveness, but it isn't. Antler bulk and the length of the tines better correlate with age, but only a postmortem examination of the wear and size of a buck's teeth can provide accurate indications. Three other hunters brought in bucks whose antlers were obviously superior to my buck's—one friend of mine had dropped an eight-point that sported a rack at least twice as big—but a rule is a rule. Here's where the Boone and Crockett Club scoring system could have most fairly put the money in the right hands. Circumstances forced me to wear a mantle of pretended shame that year for having robbed my very own neighbors of the grand sum of $28 . . . but I didn't care. I spent the money and was happy. The next year, George changed the rules to include the inside spread measurement.

"PICKED UP" AND "UNKNOWN" ANTLERS

Most of the over ten thousand antlers scores for deer, elk, moose, and caribou registered in the Boone and Crockett Club record book are listed right beside the "hunter" and "owner" columns. But, several hundred of other trophy antlers are shown there only as "picked up" or, even more mysteriously, as "unknown." Considering that the Boone and Crockett Club has set the requirement of fair chase to exemplify its commitment to sport hunting, you might wonder why they would bother to legitimize, say, a roadkill that some non-hunter might have found while looking for strawberries.

Many of the registered "picked up" antlers are, in fact, from roadkills; others are from deer who were shot by hunters unable to find their quarries, or who died from more natural causes such as disease, old age, and even lightning. Several years ago, just a few miles from my country home, a high-voltage power cable broke and fell to the ground during a storm, electrocuting six deer, including two very respectable bucks. They weren't Boone and Crockett material, but you get the point here, right? Also, in 2003, two massive whitetails (the larger one grossed 180 points) were found dead by spring turkey hunters not more than seven miles from my house; they had locked antlers in combat the preceding fall and died that way. Cabela's bought the larger one's antlers.

The basic rationale behind the "picked up" policy is that a roadkill, for example, is generally understood to be a naturally wild example of its species, as opposed to those selectively bred and fed special diets in zoos or on game farms, where fair chase isn't enforced. Remember, the original purpose of the Boone and Crockett Club was to document the natural potential of various deer species to develop antlers.

Antlers of "unknown" origin usually have already been recovered from the woods in one way or another and have ended up in hotel lobbies, at antique auctions, or even out by the street in garbage cans—the antlers usually don't fit in them and knowledgeable passersby sometimes help the sanitation crews even before they arrive. Mounted heads are often found at garage sales and in used-furniture warehouses. Taxidermy methods and styling until around twenty or so years ago were rather crude, plus those mounts that hung in bars and clubhouses often have been darkly stained by tobacco fumes and not only look bad but stink, too, so usually no one wants them except dyed-in-the-wool antler hunters like you and me.

Overall, though, the fact is that the Boone and Crockett Club acknowledges and records antlers of unknown origin . . . except, by the way, antlers known to be from a zoo or high-fenced game farm. In fact, the antlers of the top two World Record non-typical whitetail deer were both "picked up." The first-place buck was found in 1981 near St. Louis, Missouri, and scored an incredible 333 $^7/_8$ inches. Right behind it in second place is the 328 $^2/_8$-inch buck that was found in Portage County, Ohio, way back in 1940. The famous Lovestuen buck that was killed in 2003 by a teenaged muzzle-loader in Monroe County, Iowa, was actually a

This spectacular example of drop-tined antlers was "picked-up" in 1974 and scored 196 $^3/_8$ inches.

good 21 inches shorter than the second-place buck, but it is billed as the "Number 1 non-typical whitetail killed by a hunter" in many magazine articles, and you sort of lose perspective about its being ranked in third place.

So, you don't need to have actually killed a trophy deer yourself to have your name in the Boone and Crockett Club record book. You just have to be extremely lucky at finding a dead deer with antlers still

intact, or at being at the right garage sale at the right time when someone who doesn't realize the current value of large antlers is getting rid
of an old rack. According to one fellow who makes his living buying
and selling antlers online, his three main sources of antlers are people
moving into smaller homes, estate sales, and divorce settlements . . . or
any combination thereof.

WHAT ARE THE ODDS OF FINDING
A BOONE AND CROCKETT BUCK?

Not good. Whether you're a trophy hunter, a meat-hunter, a springtime
shed-hunter, or one of those strangely quiet people who sort of hang
back in the shadows, looking for antlers in antique stores and at garage
sales, the odds that you'll ever locate a Boone and Crockett–size rack
are mighty slim. Each year in the United States, about five million deer
are killed by hunters and approximately five million more are killed by
automobiles. (Hey, these are rough numbers; we're not trying to figure
out the orbit of Jupiter.) The Boone and Crockett entries for whitetails
currently average a little over three hundred typical bucks and slightly
under two hundred non-typicals per year. So, the total is about five
hundred whitetail trophy bucks that qualify for entry for every ten million deer killed, or one trophy buck per ten thousand killed.

As you can see, your odds of ever having your name attached to a
Boone and Crockett rack are very slim indeed! Here's another way to
evaluate your chances: if you hunt for fifty years during your lifetime,
the odds that you'll ever get a Boone and Crockett whitetail trophy
improve to about one in 200. There's only one thing guaranteed here,
and that's if you stay home on the couch, your odds of success for a rare
trophy are zero. Also spelled zip, and zilch.

THE POPE AND YOUNG CLUB

The Pope and Young Club is an organization of bowhunters, and in
many ways it's patterned after the Boone and Crockett Club. In fact, it
uses the universally accepted Boone and Crockett scoring system for
trophy game animals taken by archers and maintains them in its own
database. Although the scoring methods themselves are the same for
both organizations, the minimum entry-level scores are considerably
lower for the Pope and Young Club, the reason being that an archery
hunter is operating under the combined handicaps of shorter range and
less "firepower." Also, the Pope and Young Club accepts antlers that are
still in the velvet state, because most archery seasons are open earlier in
the autumn, before the gun seasons open.

The Pope and Young Club has its own list of volunteer measurers, many of whom are also certified by the Boone and Crockett Club. A trophy deer can be registered by both organizations but only if it has fallen to an arrow. If it is taken in any other way, or has been "picked up" or is "unknown," only the Boone and Crockett Club will accept it. However, there's no time limit on when an animal can be measured and entered into the records. Many archers are often surprised to discover that their trophy that was taken twenty or thirty years ago is still a potential candidate for the record books.

MINIMUM ENTRY-LEVEL SCORES

CATEGORY	POPE AND YOUNG	BOONE AND CROCKETT
Whitetail Deer (typical)	125	160
Whitetail Deer (non-typical)	155	185
Mule Deer (typical)	145	180
Mule Deer (non-typical)	170	215
American Elk (typical)	260	360
American Elk (non-typical)	335	385
Roosevelt's Elk	225	275
Caribou, Barren Ground	325	375
Caribou, Central Canada	300	345
Caribou, Mountain	300	360
Caribou, Quebec-Labrador	325	365
Caribou, Woodland	220	265
Moose, Alaska-Yukon	170	210
Moose, Canada	135	185
Moose, Wyoming (Shiras)	125	140

THE DIFFERENCES BETWEEN TYPICAL AND NON-TYPICAL ANTLERS

The Boone and Crockett Club scoring methods are split into typical and non-typical categories for whitetail deer and Coues deer; mule deer and blacktail deer; and the American elk. (Moose, caribou, and the Roosevelt's and Tule elk are all scored as typical.) There's nothing particularly freakish about so-called non-typical antlers, but they can sometimes look remarkably different than the standard typical antlers.

Despite all the modern research that's being done on antlers these days, the reasons for non-typical growth aren't yet fully known. There's some evidence that genetics play a role in determining whether or not antlers will develop to be non-typical. One trait that seems to be passed down from generation to generation is the "drop-tines" that extend downward from a buck's main beams. As we saw in Chapter 1, injury to velvet antlers—or injuries to a deer's body, or illness—often result in misshapen development of the calcified antler, and this tendency will occur again the following year to a lesser extent, and in some cases for several years. Occasionally, this will affect both antlers. Until recently, some European wildlife managers on private estates would force non-typical growth by shooting at a buck's velvet antlers with birdshot. In the location where a shot pellet had penetrated, the antler often would have branched into a fork—and, incredibly, the opposite antler would have also forked in the same location. But most velvet injuries only affect one antler, so injury itself can't explain the existence of so many well-balanced non-typical antlers in the Boone and Crockett Club's record books.

A whitetail buck with three antlers is obviously "non-typical," whether his unusual antler formation is caused by genetics or injury. This buck, named "Three-Horn," is on display at Deerassic Park in Ohio.

From the perspective of the Boone and Crockett scoring methods, the difference between typical and non-typical is usually straightforward, and it's not difficult to decide which score sheet to use. But some of the time, the decision must be calculated rather than eyeballed. In other words, while the extremes of typical and non-typical are visually obvious to anyone familiar with the deer species, there's still a gradual continuum of one blending into the other. What's potentially at stake is the ultimate ranking in the B&C record books. This is because any formation that's not where it's supposed to be, such as a tine over 1 inch long that originates from the bottom or side of the main beam, is counted as a negative in typical scoring but is included as a positive value in non-typical scoring. So, in the case of those handsome drop-tines mentioned earlier, their total lengths would be subtracted from a typical score and added to a non-typical score. Whether this is significant is partially resolved by the higher entry-level score required for non-typical registration. If you check the blank copies of the official score sheets in the Appendix, you'll see that the "Awards" (entry) level for a typical whitetail is 160 inches, versus 185 inches for a non-typical. So, you have a 25-inch difference to work with. In this somewhatcontrived example, if there were no other abnormalities and the rack had otherwise scored somewhere between those two entry-level numbers (not including the tines), how you count the drop-tines might determine whether you even get in the door. For much higher-scoring antlers, the ultimate overall ranking could be determined by which category is selected. Of course, in nearly all cases, that would be decided or recommended by the official Boone and Crockett scorer.

Artisans who make things from antlers probably don't care very much whether the antlers they're working with are technically typical or non-typical, but that sort of distinction is extremely important to a collector of antlers or a trophy hunter. There's just something about non-typical antlers that makes some people want to put them on display rather than cut them into knife handles or coffee table legs. To some extent, the freak-show aspect of unusual antlers comes into play, but there's more to it than that, I think. For one thing, as the table on the next page shows, non-typical antlers are far too common to be considered freaks. After all, approximately one out of three trophy whitetail antler racks is non-typical, and one out of four elk and mule deer antler racks also is. (There aren't any Boone and Crockett non-typical categories for caribou and moose, and I was told by Julie Houk, the club's director of publications, that there had not yet been a need shown for those species.)

One thing about non-typical antlers that strikes me is that if they only occurred adjacent to nuclear-waste sites, we would just *know* that something was wrong. Yet, when many antler fanatics look at the convoluted twists and numerous spires of high-scoring non-typical antlers, they see only beauty therein. My personal take on non-typicals is based on my faith in the principle that "form follows function," or should, anyway, and in the case of non-typical antlers, it often doesn't. OK, there's a case to be made that drop-tines give additional protection to a combatting buck's eyes and throat. Beyond that, though, I personally just don't get it.

TYPICAL AND NON-TYPICAL ANTLERS IN THE
BOONE AND CROCKETT DATABASE, 1994–2004

CATEGORY	TOTAL NUMBER OF ANTLERS	PERCENT TYPICAL	PERCENT NON-TYPICAL
Whitetail	3,828	65.6	34.4
Elk (American)	350	73.7	26.3
Mule Deer	615	76.7	23.3
Coues Deer	158	79.8	20.2
Columbia Blacktail	260	98.5	1.5
Sitka Blacktail	57	100.0	0.0

In the table above, note that non-typical antlers are apparently rare-to-nonexistent in the two mule deer subspecies (Columbia and Sitka blacktails). This may have something to do with the smaller sizes of these deer. In larger whitetails and mule deer, drop-tines and other unusual features are the major characteristics of non-typical racks, but they generally don't appear until the buck matures and can develop a larger rack. In subsequent years, as the buck ages, the drop-tines become more exaggerated, so it's believed that this trait is driven by both age and genetics. Considering the near-absence of non-typical racks in the smaller blacktail subspecies, however, it could be that mere size matters more than age. In other words, it seems possible that non-typical antlers are rare in young bucks not because the bucks are young, but because their antlers are still relatively small.

Take the B&C scores from 1994 to 2004. The top typical whitetail during those ten years was scored at 204 $^2/_8$ inches, and the smaller Coues deer was only 143. The top typical mule deer sported a 216 $^2/_8$-inch rack, while the two smaller blacktail subspecies carried scores of only 170 $^1/_8$ (Columbia) and 121 $^6/_8$ (Sitka). What's at stake in this discussion is whether non-typical antlers are actually more "normal" than we think. Consider this: Human males don't start growing whiskers until they become teenagers, at which time facial hair is normal. In that example, age defines what "normal" is. On the other hand, if whiskers only grew on human males who weighed over, say, 150 pounds regardless of age, then weight would be the determining factor. As I see it, non-typical features are "normal" only on whitetails and mule deer with larger antlers.

TROPHY ANTLERS BY SPECIES

I used the Boone and Crockett online database (see page 74) to develop the table on page 67. This breaks down the percentages of deer species and subspecies that were registered in the B&C record book from 1994 to 2004. I used that recent ten-year period to better establish where the divisions currently are, rather than include possible trends existing over a longer period. It's probably reasonable to assume that this listing is a very close approximation of the proportions of antlered game that are annually tagged by hunters in North America. You might think that it also indicates the relative availabilities of antlers for our various hobbies, crafts, and similar addictions (including shed-hunting) and that it revealed the balance of supply and demand to be seen here.

This is not always the case, however. In the table, the whitetail deer is shown (at 56.8 percent) to be by far the most common of the antlered species, which seems reasonable. In fact, there are more whitetails than all the other mule deer, moose, caribou, and elk combined. At the bottom of the list, I was surprised to find that elk totaled only 6.7 percent, the lowest percentage of all, way behind even moose and caribou. So, I queried the Rocky Mountain Elk Foundation about it, and my e-mail got passed around among the staff for general opinions.

One response (from a hunter) pointed out that elk are just plain hard to get close enough to shoot at. He wrote that when a hunter steps into elk territory and the elk can smell him, they just run away until they're in a different zip code. On the other hand, whitetail deer just tend to hide wherever they happen to be and are easier to hunt. And with caribou, all you have to do is hide behind a rock while the herd files past you, and the hard part is deciding which of many big bulls to shoot. Another fellow suggested that because the ten-year period I'd used coincided with a time when most of the western states had been on a mission to reduce elk populations, the actual number of trophy-class elk had been substantially reduced. Yet another theory was that because a bull elk's antlers don't grow to full size until age seven or eight, there might be an ongoing decline in the average ages of the bulls that is resulting in lower Boone and Crockett scores. (For whitetail deer, ages of four or five years are most common in the trophy classes, with many reaching entry-level scoring at only three years of age.)

At any rate, from the perspective of an antler fanatic, elk antlers are rather common and are easy to find on the market. This is partly because they are roughly ten times as big as deer antlers, so a little goes a long way for carvers and fabricators. Ironically, although twice as many caribou and moose are registered than are elk in the record books, their antlers are considerably less common among antler artisans.

The subspecies of the deer, moose, caribou, and elk are also shown on the table to provide a broader view of potential antler sources. The

Coues deer is actually a slightly smaller version of a whitetail, just as the Columbia and Sitka blacktails are small cousins of mule deer. The differentiating aspect (other than size) is that they exist only in the western U.S., in regions defined by Boone and Crockett. Unless you're a collector, there's no reason to think of their antlers as being anything other than small deer antlers. The same sort of regional differentiation applies to the subspecies of moose and caribou. All of them, from the Barren Ground caribou to the Tule elk, are handled and scored separately by Boone and Crockett. Again using the database, here are the relative rankings according to size:

Whitetail
The antlers of the Coues subspecies are only about two-thirds the size of the larger whitetail's. Put another way, by B&C scoring standards, the entry level for the Coues deer is five *feet* shorter than for the whitetail.

Mule Deer
The Columbia blacktail's antlers are considerably larger than the Sitka's, but the very largest Columbia antlers would barely make it beyond their big cousin mule deer's entry level of 180 inches. On the other hand, the Sitka blacktail would have a hard time winning an ordinary whitetail buck contest at my local gas station.

Moose
Hardly a contest. The farther north you go, the bigger the antlers of the moose subspecies get. The Alaskan moose is significantly bigger than the Canadian moose (but probably not as polite), and the Canadian moose is again that much larger than the Wyoming moose (but not as loud in public).

Caribou
The Mountain caribou definitely has the largest antlers and the Woodland caribou the smallest. The difference between the two of them is significant: roughly seven *feet* of antler measurements! The other subspecies, the Barren Ground, Central Canada, and Quebec-Labrador, are clustered together in the high middle.

Elk
The American elk is larger than the Roosevelt's by roughly 30 to 40 inches. That same difference pushes the Tule elk into third place, but you wouldn't want to get on an elevator with one. "Going up?"

PERCENTAGE OF ANTLERS REGISTERED WITH
BOONE AND CROCKETT CLUB, 1994–2004, BY SUBSPECIES

WHITETAIL DEER

Whitetail Deer (typical) 35.8

Whitetail Deer (non-typical) 18.7

Coues Deer (typical) 1.8

Coues Deer (non-typical) 0.5

Total Whitetail: 56.8

MULE DEER

Mule Deer (typical) 6.7

Mule Deer (non-typical) 2.0

Columbia Blacktail (typical) 3.6

Columbia Blacktail (non-typical) 0.1

Sitka Blacktail (typical) 0.8

Sitka Blacktail (non-typical) 0.0

Total Mule Deer: 13.2

MOOSE

Shiras/Wyoming Moose 4.2

Canada Moose 3.8

Alaska-Yukon Moose 3.9

Total Moose: 11.9

CARIBOU

Mountain Caribou 1.9

Woodland Caribou 1.8

Barren Ground Caribou 3.0

Central Canada Caribou 3.2

Quebec-Labrador Caribou 1.5

Total Caribou: 11.4

ELK

American Elk (typical) 3.7

American Elk (non-typical) 1.3

Roosevelt's Elk (typical) 1.5

Tule Elk (typical) 0.2

Total Elk: 6.7

(Number of Racks: 7,200)

HOW TO MEASURE AND SCORE A TYPICAL WHITETAIL RACK

I think that all of us antler fanatics should have at least a rough under-standing of how antlers are scored . . . even the carvers and the artisans. One of the main reasons for my belief can be found in Chapter 2, where we've seen that antlers for crafts and antlers for display are generally priced by two different criteria, the one for craft antlers being sheer weight, and the other, for collectors, being the Boone and Crockett score. I personally have a working knowledge of whitetail antlers and can tell at a glance whether a rack is worthy of a braggart's display or valuable only if cut into small pieces. On the other hand, there hasn't been a moose in my backyard since before the last Ice Age, and my lack of hands-on experience with moose antlers makes me vulnerable to believing that they all are worth a fortune just because they're so dog-gone big. Today, online advertisements for display and collectors' antlers include the Boone and Crockett score as surely as a car ad would list the engine's horsepower. If you understand the rudiments of official scoring, you'll be better able to decide if the price seems right. One thing you definitely don't ever want to do is to machine a set of ten-thousand-dollar antlers into knife handles!

In the Appendix beginning on page 193, you'll find the official Boone and Crockett Club score sheets for all North American deer species. Each sheet describes the requirements for an accurate measurement. For example, a rack should air-dry with the skull or skull plate attached unrestrained for sixty days before measuring begins. Official measuring is done with a flexible steel tape, $1/4$ inch wide and marked to the nearest $1/8$ inch. (All fractions are shown in eighths; a half-inch is written as $4/8$, not $1/2$.) There are also certain measurements that are officially specified but have nothing to do with the final score. These include the number of points, the tip-to-tip spread, and the greatest outside spread, which are called for just to help characterize the appearance of the rack.

What follows is the series of measurements used to determine a Boone and Crockett Score. It is intended for those folks who just want to get a rough idea of what this scoring thing is all about, and if you're doing this just for fun, go right ahead and do it your way . . . but don't use the name of Boone and Crockett in vain.

Record these measurements:
1. Length of left main beam, measured along outside edge
2. Length of right main beam, measured along outside edge
3. Greatest inside spread between beams. (If the spread measure-ment exceeds the length of the longest beam, use the longest beam for the spread measurement.)

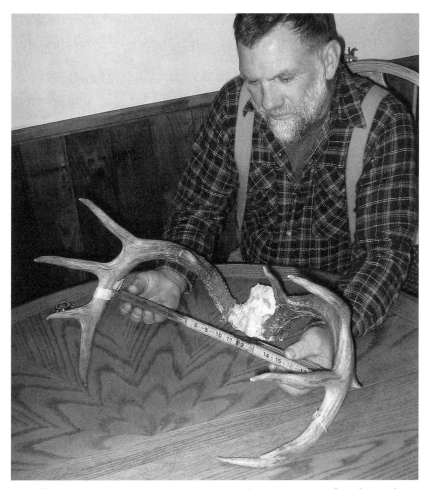

For official scoring purposes, the inside spread measurement of a whitetail rack can't be longer than the length of the longest main beam. If it is, the beam's length is recorded in place of the spread measurement, and the excess of the spread is subtracted from the total score.

4. Length of all normal (typical) points longer than the width and at least 1 inch long
5. Circumference at smallest place between burr and first point
6. Circumference at smallest place between first and second point
7. Circumference at smallest place between second and third point
8. Circumference at smallest place between third and fourth point or, if no fourth point, halfway between third point and beam tip

Add measurements 1 though 8. This will be the "Gross Score."

Now record the following:
9. If the inside spread was longer than the longest beam, the difference in inches
10. The total lengths of all non-typical points that originate from any place except the tops of the main beams. Also include lengths of any points over eight per antler. (Note: If the deer is to be considered a non-typical, the sum of all these point lengths is not recorded here but added to the Gross Score.)
11. Add the lengths of all points on the left side. Separately, add all the right-side point lengths together. Then subtract one sum from the other and record the difference.
12. The difference between the sums of the four right and four left circumferences
13. The difference between the two main beam lengths

Add measurements 9 though 13. This will be the "Negative Sum."

To get the unofficial Boone and Crockett "Net Score," subtract the Negative Sum from the Gross Score.

As you can see, the Boone and Crockett scoring system places a high value on symmetry and a long-tined, "basket-shaped" rack. There are perhaps a hundred or so whitetail antlers recorded in the database that were contenders for world-record status in terms of raw mass and size, except that they were slightly flawed in terms of symmetry and overall shape and consequently were bumped down to lower placements.

If your unofficial score comes close to or above the minimum score for entry into the Boone and Crockett record books, you can contact the Records Department by phone at (406) 542-1888, ext. 204 or by e-mail at bcclub@boone-crockett.org for a list of Official Measurers for your area. These designated people are unpaid volunteers, but in order for a trophy to be registered by the club, it must be measured by them. There's a modest fee to have your trophy score registered.

The Records Program includes trophies taken by bow, rifle, handgun, and other methods. The Boone and Crockett scores for antlered game killed by bow and arrow can additionally be registered with the Pope and Young organization, using that same score—although under some circumstances, the P&Y officials might want to have their own certified scorers repeat the measuring and calculating.

SCORING SINGLE SHED ANTLERS

The main problem with scoring single antlers such as sheds is that there's no "inside spread" to be measured. Yet, shed-hunters are just as enthusiastic as the rest of us to determine a score for their antlers. In response to this, the North American Shed Hunters Club has established a formal measuring system and keeps the resulting scores in an official record book. NASHC has been authorized to base their measuring and scoring system on Boone and Crockett's. The NASHC score is simply a total of the length of the main beam, the lengths of each tine over 1 inch, and the circumferences of the main beam between each tine and the next. You can do these measurements to determine whether it would be worth your while to have the antler officially scored for possible entry into the annual NASHC record book. Here are the minimum net scores that you need to attain to qualify; they approximate the Boone and Crockett minimum standards for two-antlered deer.

NASHC ENTRY-LEVEL SCORES

SPECIES	TYPICAL	NON-TYPICAL
Whitetail	60 inches	70 inches
Columbia Blacktail	50	60
Coues Deer	30	35
Sitka Blacktail	30	35
Mule Deer	65	75
Canada Moose	50	NA
Yukon Moose	60	NA
Shiras Moose	40	NA
American Elk	135	150
Roosevelt's Elk	100	NA
Tule Elk	90	100
Mountain Caribou	150	NA
Woodland Caribou	100	NA
Barren Ground Caribou	150	NA
Central Canada Caribou	125	NA
Quebec-Labrador Caribou	150	NA

If your unofficial scoring indicates that a certain antler might qualify for NASHC registration, then you can contact the organization at NASHC02@yahoo.com for a list of official scorers. Official scoring sheets for each of these species are available at no cost and can be printed from the NASHC website. The entry guidelines and instructions are included.

**Records of
North American
Big Game**

BOONE AND CROCKETT CLUB®
OFFICIAL SCORING SYSTEM FOR NORTH AMERICAN BIG GAME

	MINIMUM SCORES			TYPICAL
	AWARDS	ALL-TIME		WHITETAIL AND COUES' DEER
whitetail	160	170		
Coues'	100	110		

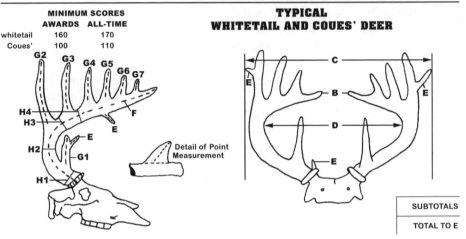

Detail of Point Measurement

SUBTOTALS

TOTAL TO E

A typical whitetail rack as it appears on the Boone and Crockett scoring sheet. Note that the positive valves apply only to tines that point upward from the main beams.

To satisfy your own personal curiosity, you can calculate from a single antler a rough estimate of what the full, two-antlered Boone and Crockett score might have been for the buck by multiplying your single-shed score by 2 and then adding to that result your best guess as to what the inside spread might have been. For example, if the single antler scored 50 points and the imaginary inside spread might have been 20 inches, you'd have 50 × 2 = 100, and 100 + 20 = a score of 120 inches. Not bad! (But not great, either.)

SCORING ANTLERS ONLINE

Now that you know how the measuring and final calculating is done, you might want to check your results with the "Online Scoring" section of the Boone and Crockett Club's website (www.boone-crockett.org). This free feature does all the figuring once you've entered the measured data. The website provides you with a list of all the species of North American game animals for which scoring has been done—everything from bison to walrus. You can select (for example) "non-typical white-

Records of North American Big Game

BOONE AND CROCKETT CLUB®
OFFICIAL SCORING SYSTEM FOR NORTH AMERICAN BIG GAME

MINIMUM SCORES			NON-TYPICAL
	AWARDS	ALL-TIME	WHITETAIL AND COUES' DEER
whitetail	185	195	
Coues'	105	120	

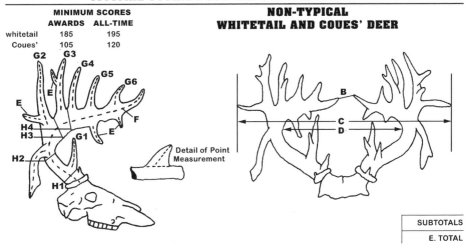

Detail of Point Measurement

SUBTOTALS
E. TOTAL

A non-typical whitetail rack as it appears on the Boone and Crockett scoring sheet. In addition to drop-tines and other tines that sprout in various directions from unusual locations on the main beams, there is considerable forking, which results in a larger number of measurable points.

tail" to bring up the correct antler score sheet, which is accompanied by a sketch of the front and side views with lettered descriptions for where measurements are to be taken. (Remember, the "outside spread" and the "tip-to-tip" measurements are for characterization purposes only and aren't included in the actual score.) You can then scroll down to the tabulation section, enter the data, press a button, and get your final score. This program takes care of all the necessary additions and subtractions and, at the end, also offers you the opportunity (still free) to print out an "Unofficial Score Chart" that contains all the measured data and the final score. (If you use the right high-quality printer paper, your unofficial chart could even be suitable for framing!) Blank score sheets are also available in PDF format.

You can even score single shed antlers with the Boone and Crockett online scoring feature. I played around with the program to see how it could be made to work with a single antler, and here's the procedure I found: Enter all the data for the one antler (number of points, lengths of main beam and tines, and circumferences) in the appropriate boxes. If a tine is non-typical, then enter it in the non-typical box. Then copy that data exactly for the other antler, as though you had a perfectly symmetrical rack. For inside and outside spreads and tip-to-tip measurements, just type in a zero. A score will appear . . . but it will be double the true value for the single antler, and you'll have to divide it by 2.

Now, to have some fun, you can repeat this online scoring and then guesstimate what the inside spread would have been on the original deer. As a rough rule of thumb, the inside spread of a well-balanced rack is slightly shorter than the length of one beam. Enter your guess to find what the full rack might have scored.

THE BOONE AND CROCKETT CLUB DATABASE

For fifty bucks a year (little play on words there), you can subscribe to the online Boone and Crockett Club database. That's what I did so I could generate the antler data for many of the graphs and tables that appear in this book. The database is a treasure that includes all the recorded antler data going back, in the case of whitetail deer, to 1830. Yes, in 1830 (not a typo), Arthur Young of McKean County, Pennsylvania, shot a typical whitetail buck that scored 175 $^4/_8$ inches and became the earliest recorded deer . . . although it wasn't officially scored for over a hundred years! The first issue of *Records of North American Big Game* wasn't published until 1932, but even then, the rankings were based only on subjective standards. It wasn't until 1950 that the Boone and Crockett Club adopted the measuring system that is still in effect today.

The database gives you so many search options that it's difficult sometimes to make yourself leave the keyboard for supper or bed. With this information at my fingertips, I was able to determine, for example, how many (and which) of the whitetail and mule deer racks, both typical and non-typical, are presently owned by Cabela's and Bass Pro Shops. Particularly useful for this book, the program let me rank antler scores by year over a period of time so that I could detect trends in the median scores (see Chapter 10). For example: Are non-typical whitetail deer nationwide decreasing as a percentage of total whitetails? (Yes.) And, are typical whitetail deer antler scores getting smaller as the years go by? (Yes.) Using the database I also found that the only two B&C whitetails ever registered from Chautauqua County, New York, where I live, were obtained very recently, in 1998 and 2002, by two hunters who live in the same small town, only seven miles from my home. Maybe this means that the next entry could have my name on it?

The possibilities continue. If you were interested, for some strange reason that only another antler fanatic could fathom, what the ranking and range was of the inside spreads for all 5,265 typical whitetail deer currently registered, you'd be able to determine that the widest was 32 inches, and the narrowest was a mere 13 ^{4}/$_8$ inches. Let me go through that again, adding a few details for perspective. To repeat, the widest rack had a 32-inch spread (Kansas, 1991) and scored at 197 ^{2}/$_8$, while the rack right behind it, in second place at 30 ^{4}/$_8$ inches (Colorado, 1990) scored a considerably lower 174 ^{5}/$_8$.

Now let's go to the bottom of the width-ranking list, 5,265th place. As I said a moment ago, the narrowest spread there was only 13 ^{4}/$_8$ inches (Texas, 2000); it scored 163 ^{2}/$_8$, which is barely beyond the Boone and Crockett entry level. But get this: the second-to-last inside spread of 13 ^{7}/$_8$ inches (Saskatchewan, 1999) scored 173 ^{1}/$_8$, which is almost identical to the second-from-the-top Boone and Crockett score of 174 ^{5}/$_8$. This implies that the inside spread is possibly the most variable of all the characteristics of deer antlers.

THE MILO HANSON BUCK

There are only 128 typical whitetail deer registered by the Boone and Crockett Club that have been scored at 190 inches or higher, and as the chart below shows, the number of bucks goes down as the score rises. Milo Hanson, a farmer in Saskatchewan, shot the world-record typical whitetail buck on his own property in 1993. The buck was scored at a phenomenal 213 ^{5}/$_8$ inches, over 7 inches larger than the Jordan buck that had been dropped seventy-nine years earlier, in 1914.

Although the Hanson buck's inside spread of 27 ^{2}/$_8$ inches is very impressive, it ranks only 32nd in the overall typical whitetail category; at 28 ^{4}/$_8$ inches, the main beams are several hundred placements down on the Boone and Crockett list. The new champion buck technically has six points on one side and eight on the other, but it is basically a classic 6x6 with a couple of very small tines over 1 inch long on one side . . . again, far below where you'd expect the top buck overall to be. There are literally several hundred whitetail bucks registered that have more points, but where Milo's buck begins to really shine is in the lengths of some of those tines: six of them are between 11 and 14 inches long.

Another clincher for the buck's top position is the near-perfect symmetry of the left and right antlers, which results in a negative subtraction of only 3 ^{1}/$_8$ inches from gross to net score. The final triumph of the Milo Hanson rack is its simple conformity to the Boone and Crockett

Frequency of Typical Whitetail Scores

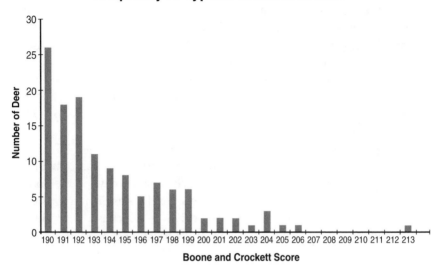

Boone and Crockett Score

Club's ideal "basket" shape, where the inside spread does not exceed the length of the longest beam. (If it does, the credit for inside spread measurement is reduced to the longest beam length.) Hanson's champion buck came within only 1 ¼ inches of being that "ultimate basket."

The Milo Hanson buck was determined to be only 4 ½ years old, so it obviously had superior genes for growing antlers. Until recently, it was believed that most bucks grew their biggest antlers at that age, but more recent studies have shown that a buck doesn't reach its optimum potential for antler development until age 7 ½ after the full muscle and bone growth has been attained. So, it's possible that the Hanson buck would have grown even higher-scoring antlers during the next three years. But, maybe not. There are indications that as any buck and its antlers increase in size, so does the propensity for non-typical antler growth, and if that were to have happened, the developing abnormalities would have been cause for extra subtractions from the total score. The two small points on one side that are scarcely visible in photos might be an indication that abnormal growths would soon be showing up in subsequent years. Or, maybe not.

BOONE AND CROCKETT WORLD RECORD HOLDERS
On the following pages are some photographs, courtesy of the Boone and Crockett Club, of the top-scoring racks in several categories, including the Hanson buck.

TYPICAL WHITETAIL DEER

SCORE: 213 $5/8$

LOCATION: Biggar, SK

HUNTER: Milo N. Hanson

OWNER: Milo N. Hanson

DATE: 1993

NON-TYPICAL
    WHITETAIL DEER

SCORE: 333 $7/8$

LOCATION:
    St. Louis County, MO

HUNTER: Picked Up

OWNER: MO Department
    of Conservation

DATE: 1981

TYPICAL MULE DEER

SCORE: 226 $^4/_8$

LOCATION:
Dolores County, CO

HUNTER: Doug Burris Jr.

OWNER: Cabela's, Inc.

DATE: 1972

TYPICAL AMERICAN ELK

SCORE: 442 $^5/_8$

LOCATION:
White Mtns.,
AZ

HUNTER:
Alonzo Winters

OWNER:
Alan C. Ellsworth

DATE: 1968

WYOMING (SHIRAS)
   MOOSE

SCORE: 205 $^4/_8$

LOCATION:
   Green River Lake, WY

HUNTER: John M. Oakley

OWNER:
   Jackson Hole Museum

DATE: 1952

CENTRAL CANADA
   BARREN GROUND
   CARIBOU

SCORE: 433 $^4/_8$

LOCATION:
   Humpy Lake, NT

HUNTER: Donald J. Hotter III

OWNER: Bass Pro Shops

DATE: 1994

5

THE MEDICAL BENEFITS
OF VELVET ANTLERS

DO ANTLERS *REALLY* MAKE YOU HORNY?

Let's get right to the point. Do antlers make you horny? Besides the play on words, the quickest answer is, well . . . yeah, maybe—but the whole subject is a lot more complicated than a simple yes or no can accurately address. Antlers in one form or another have a worldwide reputation as an aphrodisiac—an enhancer of sexual desire and performance—and most westerners claim to "know" that this is what the Chinese and other Asians believe. Again, that is only partly true; the subject here also begs to be expanded and explained.

There are two things that make the idea of antler aphrodisiacs intuitively appealing. The first is the symbolic nature of antlers—it's the male deer that wears them for the obvious purpose of warding off other males so that he alone can breed the receptive female. Secondly, female deer are, in fact, more attracted to those bucks that have bigger antlers. Now, I won't take *that* subject too far here, except to say that the growth of larger-size antlers is indeed a strong indication of good health, good genes, and a better chance of winning a prize in superiority in any pushing contest with a smaller-antlered buck. There's even some evidence that a buck that has lost the right to breed in such a contest will actually grow slightly smaller antlers the following year. I wonder . . . If we men had leg-size bones growing out of our heads, would women find us more desirable . . . or would they just think we looked silly?

Velvet antler's role as an often-effective treatment for certain conditions led the first western physicians who had begun studying eastern medicine to classify it as an aphrodisiac. Don't forget: just being in good health is often the best thing for your libido. However quaintly or condescendingly that initial assessment may have been intended, some modern researchers now claim that it has sidetracked the serious scientific investigations of antlers' broad spectrum of therapeutic uses.

Antlers in velvet are sensitive to touch due to a fully developed nerve system. They begin sprouting in early summer, fed by an abundant supply of blood that can circulate all the way to the tips of the antlers.

There is a growing body of evidence that antler, if prepared correctly for market, contains many medically valuable compounds—and more are being discovered every year as interest in the subject grows. There is already a growing demand in the United States for antler in various forms as health-food supplements ("nutraceuticals") for athletic performance and as a treatment for arthritis.

There really is something very special about the ability of deer species to grow antlers every year that suggests potentially beneficial uses for humankind. (Herein, I again quote Dr. George Bubenik, MD, Professor of Zoology at the University of Guelph, Ontario, the source of almost everything that's scientifically meaningful in this book.) Antlers in velvet grow at a very rapid rate—in the larger-antlered caribou and elk, for example, at almost $3/4$ inch per day. That's the fastest growth of appendages in the animal kingdom. When you consider that no other mammal species can regenerate a lost organ or limb, the fact that a deer can annually regrow antlers consisting in the velvet stage of live bone, cartilage, blood, nerves, embryonic tissues, skin, and even hair means it's not too much of a stretch to think that there is something happening there that might be of benefit to us. It is already known and well documented by western scientists that live, growing ("fresh") velvet antler contains peptides, hormones, enzymes, growth factors and their derivatives, and the vitamins associated with tissue growth and healing.

ANTLERS IN EASTERN MEDICINE

Velvet antler has been one of the more important components of Asian medicine for more than two thousand years, and there is some archeological evidence of antler being used for curing illness going back as far as four thousand years. Today, China, Hong Kong, Taiwan, Singapore, Korea, and Japan are the greatest consumers of velvet antler, most of which comes from New Zealand, the United States, and Canada. In the West, there has been a reluctance to accept the widely ranging claims of health and well-being attributed to velvet antler by Asians. That's chiefly because of the lack of the scientific proof. According to various Asian sources, velvet antler nutraceuticals can cure or improve the effects of aging, anemia, diabetes, cancer, dwarfism, fatigue, gastric ulcers, hypertension, high cholesterol, insanity, infertility, insomnia, liver disease, memory loss, muscle weakness, osteoarthritis, osteomyelitis, osteoporosis, stress, thrombosis, weak immune system, even whiplash, and, finally (you were waiting for this, right?), impotence. Yes, impotence; that's how we got on this subject in the first place.

While it's probably wise to be skeptical of any claim for a medicine that says it can do everything, some say we westerners, especially Americans, view the dark cave of illness with our flashlights too tightly focused. For example, until the late 1990s, aspirin was considered good only for headaches and other mild pain; then daily doses of baby aspirin were discovered to be a virtual miracle drug for preventing heart disease in men. Similarly, western scientists are beginning to find more potential health benefits from velvet antlers than even the Asians might have claimed.

There's an interesting twist to this picture of a western science evolving from the more holistic world of eastern medicine. It has to do with differences in the ways in which the antler is prepared for use. Boiling in water and drying under heat are the traditional Asian methods for extracting the medically valuable components from velvet antler. However, in these harsh, high-temperature processes, much if not all of the "goodness" is lost, according to modern chemical analysis. The irony here, therefore, is that many of the Asian claims of good health from velvet antlers are based on components that have literally been watered down, if not completely destroyed. Recently developed western methods for processing antler for research include using either alcohol or water at low temperatures. Rapid freeze-drying is also used on fresh antler. In either case, the research and analysis are done on velvet that is basically fresh off the deer. Modern chemical analysis techniques are easily able to detect the various beneficial components of these extracts, but not in heat-treated antlers. More effective means of extraction, preservation, and packaging are not yet standard practice among commercial processors, but they will need to be in order for velvet to be marketed more successfully on American shelves. The full scientific potential of velvet will probably have been realized in the lab before that happens, though.

MEDICAL RESEARCH WITH ANTLERS

Over the last few decades, numerous studies have been performed exploring the possible medical uses of velvet antler. Research into the effects on wound healing in rats is currently being expanded, based on early favorable results. The long-range goal is to provide assistance to both human medical and veterinary practices in the care and treatment of surgical patients and accident victims. Another project seeks to determine the possible effect of elk velvet on blood cholesterol levels and clotting disorders. This was inspired in part by the observation that as a velvet antler's natural death approaches prior to shedding, the supply of blood to the antler is shut off by constriction of the arteries. This is very similar to a human "myocardial infarction"—a heart attack—which is caused primarily by a blood clot that plugs an artery already narrowed by cholesterol deposits. So, a deer has the amazing ability to produce an "antler attack," on purpose, every year, and in the same place on its body.

Tests have also been conducted to determine the effect of antler extract on athletic performance. Many of them involve the measurement of resistance to fatigue and stress in laboratory rats, for the simple reason that there's no placebo effect: they aren't fooled by self-delusion, as humans often are when they take a pill. In an experiment to test the effect of velvet extract on swimming endurance, untreated lab rats could swim for only 17.8 minutes, but those treated with 50 mg/kg/day (dosage per rat weight per day) for only five days swam for 48.4 minutes, and those rats that were given a double dose could swim for 69.2 minutes.

In a preliminary study for rheumatoid arthritis (an auto-immune disease of the cartilage that connects the bones) research program, forty patients were treated in a double-blind, placebo-controlled trial that showed that use of velvet antler correlated with twice the rate of improvement within only six weeks of treatment. Recently, it was determined that an extract from velvet antlers exhibited antifungal properties against *Candida albicans*, which is the main fungus responsible for vaginal and toenail infections and intestinal difficulties.

Velvet antler has been successfully used in bone grafts in the laboratory. Two exceptional properties make it particularly suitable for this purpose: its rapid growth abilities and the embryonic stem cells in its tissue. Growing velvet naturally contains a great amount of growth-supporting factors for blood vessel development and nerve, skin, hair, and bone growth, and it even improves the way in which a healing fracture can take advantage of a foreign substance instead of rejecting it. George Bubenik has gone on record saying that, thanks to the presence of embryonic stem cells in velvet antlers, the current research being done on the antler growth of whitetail deer may one day enable humans to regrow severed fingers and limbs. These stem cells can differentiate into skin, blood vessels, cartilage, and bone, just as human stem cells do in utero. Deer antlers are remarkably useful for this kind of medical and biochemical research for several reasons, including the ability to sample growing bone tissues without having to kill or otherwise damage an ordinary laboratory animal. And the following year, the same "lab deer" can grow another set of antlers.

It's also possible that antlers may be helpful in treating the crippling disease osteoporosis, which is particularly common in postmenopausal women. Antler growth in deer is so rapid that there's not enough time for a buck's vegetarian diet to adequately provide all the calcium and phosphorous needed for antler development. So, the buck robs its own body for most of the missing supplements: the deer's system removes what it requires from the skeleton, particularly the ribs, sternum, and vertebrae. This process of demineralization resembles osteoporosis. Deer, however, can quickly replace the lost calcium when the hardening of the antlers has been completed. Humans can't. Scientists assume that this process involves hormonal regulation involving the parathyroid gland, but the actual mechanics by which the bone densities are increased are not yet known. Work is continuing in the United States and Canada to find a cure for osteoporosis using antler and deer bone materials.

The following lists just some of the antler-related scientific discoveries quoted in a 2003 technical presentation by Dr. George Bubenik. All of the results cited below were obtained in double-blind, randomized, placebo-controlled studies.

- Determined that fresh antler extract is effective in promoting growth when fed to laboratory rats. This also indicated that some metabolic properties of velvet survive the digestive process. (Suttie and Haines, 2001)
- Evidence found of production of alkaline phosphates and tri-iodothyronine in growing antlers. (Bubenik et al., 1987)
- Discovered production of Vitamin D3 in velvet antler tissues. (Sempere et al., 1989)
- Determined that the extracellular matrices in growing antlers consist of polysaccharide glycosaminoglycans linked to protein. Subsequently, discovered that extract made from the velvet antler was effective in the treatment of osteoporosis in animals. (Sunwoo and Sim, 2001)
- Growth factors for epidermis (Ko et al., 1986) and for nerve development (Huo et al., 1997) detected, along with fibroblast activity (Sunwoo et al., 1997).
- Found that parathyroid-related peptide plays a role in the regulation of certain types of bone formation. (Price and Faucheux, 2001)
- Experiments with laboratory rats indicated that skin and hair regeneration is enhanced by the application of velvet extract as compared with an ordinary saline solution. This preliminary "pilot" study (Bubenik, circa 1979) was later supported by the discovery of certain skin and hair growth hormones (Ko et al., 1986 and Sunwoo et al., 1997).
- Found that velvet antler extract accelerated the formation of chondrocytes and osteoblasts (bone cells), and facilitated the healing of fractures in laboratory mice. (Zhoa et al. 1999)
- Found that velvet antlers themselves (not as an extract, but as actual pieces surgically removed) may serve as potential bone grafting material for human injuries. Unlike synthetic materials, which have no resemblance to natural bone, velvet antler has many physical characteristics consistent with human alveolar bones. (Ongaro, 2001)

So . . . where is the money coming from for all these important research projects? Well, as it turns out, various organizations of elk farmers are major contributors; we'll see why in a minute. I personally have no problem with that. The results of the work that has been done so far are so promising, and so fully based on scientific fact, that perhaps we all should consider reaching deep into our pockets to contribute!

VELVET ANTLERS YES, HARD ANTLERS . . . NO

That's right, there's no scientific evidence that hard antlers have any beneficial effect on human health and well-being, unless they subconsciously convince a person to "get well." Old antlers are actually just bones; yes, they're full of calcium and phosphorous, but not much else. All the growth hormones and other substances needed for rapid growth are basically drained from the antler as it "dies" before being shed. Still, there is an Asian market for hard antler as an aphrodisiac, but that market began drying up (just like the antlers) in the late 1990s with the advent of pharmaceuticals that performed more effectively with less need for a hefty dose of imagination.

Actually, hard antler was used medicinally here in America a couple of centuries ago. Until early in the 1800s, the dust of hard deer antlers was the main source of ammonia, which was the chief ingredient in smelling salts. As such, it was recommended (in 1736) for fainting, swooning, heartburn, convulsions, falling sickness, hysterical fits, and . . . worms. Even today, ammonia is used to neutralize bee stings and revive people who have fainted, but it's no longer made from antlers.

GROWING ANTLERS DOWN ON THE FARM

Virtually all the velvet antler being used today in medicine and nutraceuticals is harvested from bull elk that are farmed just for that purpose. Moose aren't farmed because bulls and the cows alike tend to be belligerent and have the size and weight to back up their bad attitudes. Whitetail and mule deer, on the other hand, are too small for commercial velvet antler production, and the large rack of a whitetail buck would be worth more for sale to a collector in the hardened stage than in the velvet form.

Ironically, today there are probably far more whitetail deer than elk actually being "farmed," but generally they are kept as a hobby rather than as a commercial venture. Farming is also an option for the do-it-yourselfer who wants to process velvet for his own consumption; it's very difficult otherwise for an individual to acquire fresh antler, because the deer hunting seasons are closed in summer when all the antlered species are in velvet. In New York State, a permit to own deer is low-priced and easy to get from the Department of Agriculture. A Class B permit for keeping deer for fun is $10 per year, and a Class A permit to actually sell deer, deer products such as doe urine (used by hunters as a lure), hides, and venison is $50 per year. The only catch for either permit

Farming of whitetail deer can be done on a smaller, less expensive scale than with elk, and it is most often done just as a hobby. Shown here is Bob Turk, owner of Whitetail Splendor Deer Farms (www.whitetailsplendor.com) in Silver Creek, New York; he profits by selling deer urine to hunters for use as a lure. There are an estimated 6,000 deer farms in the US.

is that you have to obtain your deer from another deer farmer in New York, as is also the case within most of the other states. These laws exist to curb the potential for the spread of disease, particularly Chronic Wasting Disease (CWD), which causes a fatal deterioration of the animal's brain in ways similar to Mad Cow Disease. In the United States, CWD has basically been confined to the Rocky Mountain region and a few Midwestern states since the early 1970s, when it was first observed. Deer and elk farmers have been blamed in some quarters for the spread of the disease, yet in some widely separated states, only wild deer have ever been found to be infected. The recent discovery in March of 2005 of CWD in some penned whitetails in central New York State has added another dimension to the overall quest to control the spread of the disease and, ultimately, to prevent it altogether.

The money in whitetail farming is usually flowing in the wrong direction (from the farmer to the retailers of fencing and game foods), but with the recent explosion in the popularity of antlers, the sale of high-antlered bucks and even their frozen semen has turned the money tide for some deer farmers. (So far, in many states, frozen deer semen

Elk are ideal for being farmed for antlers. At the point in midsummer when their antlers are still growing about ³/₄ inch per day, bull elk are relatively docile.

can be transported across state lines even though the buck himself can't.) Still, because of the restrictions outlined above, acquiring deer for personal purposes is certainly not going to be getting any easier for a while. You can't just go into the woods and capture wild deer for two reasons: it would be incredibly difficult to do, and it's highly illegal.

In any case, most velvet comes from elk farms. These are often huge outfits covering hundreds of acres, which is consistent with their horse-size occupants. The elk farmers of the United States and Canada together produce about 60 to 90 tons per year of velvet antler. That works out to roughly eight thousand bull elk, and that's not counting the cows that are needed for adding calves to the population. New Zealand produces approximately ten times as much velvet as does North America, and China is a very close second place. As mentioned earlier, the velvet market over the last decade has been volatile; the value of velvet began falling in the late 1990s with the decline in the Asian economy and the availability of Viagra and similar pharmaceuticals. More recently, news of isolated cases of Chronic Wasting Disease resulted in South Korea

In years when the market drops for velvet elk antler, a bull such as this one will be allowed to keep his antlers until they drop in the pasture from natural shedding. The majestic rack from this six-pointer could sell for as much as the velvet would have.

(a major antler consumer) suspending all imports of antler products. For some North American farmers, the fluctuations in the economics of velvet production have resulted in many elk being processed for venison instead of antlers, but as interest in and awareness of the nutraceutical benefits of velvet grow, and as scientists make more medical breakthroughs, the price and availability of velvet antler products will likely rise again.

By the way, a disclaimer is needed here: I have no commercial interest in nor connections to any aspect of antler farming or production of antler products in any form, except that I've written this book . . . which I hope you have bought instead of borrowed! When I began writing the book, my personal opinion of velvet antler was that it was probably over-hyped and that it overlapped too much with the unsubstantiated claims made by some adherents of holistic medicine. Now, after researching the scientific journals and regularly communicating with scientists such as George Bubenik, I think that elk farming for velvet antlers has a bright future.

Harvesting Velvet Antlers

Elk antlers are removed before they can harden into the final mineralized phase of calcium and phosphorous. This is usally in June, when they're still in the growth stage, well-vascularized, naturally full of all the growth hormones and super-nutritious raw materials needed for rapid growth, well-protected against pathogens, and held aloft by a relatively soft cartilaginous structure that contains its own beneficial compounds such as glucosamine sulfate. The elk are treated with an analgesic (injections of lidocaine into the base of the antler, or a rubber ring tightly wrapped around the pedicle to numb the antler), and their

In late summer, before the bone structure of the elk antler is fully formed and while there is still a flood of growth nutrients contained within it, the farmed elk antler can be surgically removed and then prepared for human consumption as a nutraceutical.

antlers are then sawed off about an inch above the pedicle. As soon as an antler is removed, it must be turned upside-down to prevent the fluids and blood from draining out. The raw stump remaining on the bull's head must be immediately treated to slow the bleeding. This is no time to get squeamish; this is agriculture. We routinely shave the wool from sheep, accept the daily gift of chicken eggs both for food and to house the incubation of flu vaccines, and consume cow's milk and the cheese and yogurt made from it, while many post-menopausal women still use a form of estrogen that is extracted from the urine of pregnant mares. As it turns out, the most stressful part of the de-antlering process for a bull elk probably isn't the pain of having his antlers cut off, but the fear he experiences while mechanically immobilized in a chute. Measurements of the cortisol content of blood and saliva (a stress indicator) have shown that antler removal is incidental to the actual stress of being held tightly in one place.

The cut velvet antlers are frozen as soon as possible; otherwise, they would spoil as quickly as a venison steak. Later, during processing, they are dried at a low temperature, the covering of skin and hair is removed and discarded, and the remaining whole antler is ground and pulverized into a powder. The powder can be placed into capsules or made into various forms of extracts, tinctures, and ointments. In Asia, one preferred method of processing involves cutting the whole antler into thin slices that are then dried and packaged as is.

There are two things to consider about antler removal: the potential for harmful drug residues to remain in the velvet product, and the possible effects of stress on the size of future antlers. It's well known that if during the rut a wild elk bull or buck deer loses a battle or otherwise experiences the stress of prolonged competition with several other males, his antlers will usually be smaller the following year. Small antlers aren't worth as much as larger ones, so it behooves the velvet farmers to develop methods of antler removal that are as gentle as possible. Tranquilizers are a possibility, but that's easier said than done, and it presents a set of problems of its own if the drug remains in the antler.

Judging Velvet Antlers

The North American Elk Breeders Association has developed a scoring method for velvet antlers called the "Certified Weight Index." It is not just based on weight alone but several other factors, including uniformity, symmetry, and the measurements of the main beam circumferences. "Balance" is another quality that scores high; as a judging standard, the term is used to indicate a farmer's ability to decide when to cut the antlers off the elk—wait too long, and too much of the antler has become calcified. This is particularly important because the top part of a velvet antler, where the growth has been most recent (an antler calcifies from the bottom up as it matures), can be worth ten times what the lower portion would bring in the market. Judges place a high value on antler tips that are well rounded into bulbs, and they prefer that the brow and bez tines close to the butt-end are small. Ideally, the main beam diameter increases with its distance from the head. The last consideration is the degree of calcification of the antler, because the more that it has converted to pure bone, the less it's worth. Calcification is based subjectively on its overall appearance compared to other antlers with a known degree of maturity.

The Certified Weight Index is put into practice at velvet antler competitions. These events allow breeders and buyers to compare the genetic potential of a bull elk to produce large antlers and, as a stud, to produce bull calves that can grow large antlers. It costs an elk farmer as much to grow thirty pounds of antler on a thousand-pound bull as it does to produce fifteen pounds, so there is much interest in developing good breeding programs. Many thousands of dollars in stud fees can ride on the outcome of the judging, proving the extent to which antler farming, originally a hobby, has now become a growing agribusiness.

6

Mounting and Displaying Antlers

WHY DO WE PUT ANTLERS ON DISPLAY?

As I've suggested elsewhere, there's a sort of Zen detachment that evolves from the collecting, handling, and display of antlers, and if you also keep yourself up-to-date on the groundbreaking scientific news about antlers, you'll come a long way toward understanding the pure lust that many people have for them. True antler fanatics offer no apologies to anyone for the seemingly irrational attraction they have to antlers. They have no urge to explain themselves—and if someone just doesn't "get it," that's their problem.

The point is that putting antlers on display is not just a mere game of Show and Tell for grownups, although, yes, they are sometimes used that way. It's true that displaying antlers over the fireplace could be construed as an attempt at one-upmanship, but most of the time, I believe, we Antler People just like to see any antlers, even the smaller ones. Take the collectors, those who hoard antlers by the dozens and sometimes by the hundreds or more. I know a man who otherwise seems normal in every regard—he has a full-time job and a good-looking wife and smart kids—except he has a collection of over two thousand sets of antlers on display in his barn. Why are antler fanatics determined to display their collections large and small? Is it part of some personal, perhaps unconscious quest? Some people paint, photograph, or cook, all just for fun. Others, however, "go antlers," which, while not the same as "going wacko," is a point on the same sliding scale.

We need to see our antlers displayed. Consider this: the main reason that deer, elk, caribou, and moose wear antlers on their heads during the breeding season is for the purpose of display. Sure, it's true that the bucks and bulls also use them for tests of strength with other males, and sometimes, yes, one of them gets poked too hard, gets hurt, and leaves. But most of the time, a well-antlered deer can win an impending

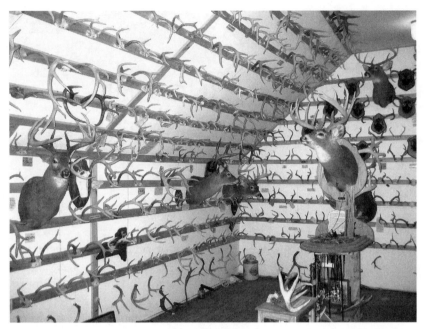

*Len Nagel's Antler Shed contains over 2,000 antlers (mostly from whitetails)
and includes several examples of antique mounts that demonstrate the art of
taxidermy prior to polyurethane forms.*

battle merely by intimidating the rival bucks with the size of his antlers.
Then they leave too. (As Woody Allen once claimed, "80 percent of success is showing up.") The females, the does and cows, are attracted by
the larger sizes of big buck antlers because large, well-formed antlers
indicate that the buck that grew them is healthier and has been able to
prove that he was the strongest competitor. My point here is that it's
normal to be impressed on a deep level by a display of antlers, whether
we are men or women . . . and we don't have to be deer to feel that way.
I verge on being ridiculous here, but please note that we don't mount
the tails of deer, while we do mount wild turkey and grouse fantails
(which are used by these game birds for courtship display). We don't
mount a buck's front leg bones either, although they're about the same
size on a big buck as the antlers and are indicators of running ability.

MOUNTING SHED ANTLERS

Many shed antlers never get mounted, usually because only one of the
buck's two antlers has been found, and having just one antler mounted
on a plaque would look silly and would hang lopsided anyway. The

missing half of the matched pair is typically either still lost in the woods or in the possession of another shed-hunter who doesn't realize that you have *his* other antler. The Boone and Crockett Club officially recognizes only those paired antlers that are still naturally attached to the same piece of original skull. The reasoning here is that the original inside spread can't otherwise ever be accurately known. The North American Shed Hunters Club similarly doesn't fool around with trying to derive a B&C-type score from two antlers that have been mechanically re-attached to a board or a skull. In fact, the official stance of NASHC on the mounting of paired shed antlers and subsequent attempts at scoring is that neither one should be a primary goal of shed-hunting. That's why the organization's display rooms contain no mounts of paired antlers. I agree with this philosophy; finding a single shed antler is a complete achievement, not just half of one.

Still, it's a great temptation to mount a matched set of shed antlers, and what you do with them in your own home is your business, right? Many shed-hunters and most deer farmers can feel absolutely certain that a set of antlers belongs to a specific buck and, consequently, desire to mount them on a plaque. But there is the question of how the antlers should be positioned, as they are no longer attached to the buck's skull plate. This is more a matter of artistic taste than accuracy. So, here are some guidelines for positioning shed antlers. Read these first and *then* consider going ahead and mounting those shed antlers yourself.

Note: Many of the guidelines and ideal measurements in this chapter are applicable to whitetail deer only.

Guidelines for Positioning Shed Antler Pairs

For whitetail deer, the distance between the burrs on the antlers at the base should never be more than 3 1/4 inches, and even that is wider than normal for all but the very largest of trophy whitetails. Larry Huffman, who owned the famous "Legendary Whitetail Collection" before it was bought by Cabela's, personally measured most of the 84 heads in that collection. He found that the distance between the burrs ranged from approximately 2 3/4 to 3 1/4 inches, which is a range of a mere 1/2 inch! Of course, smaller whitetails have smaller heads, but not by a lot. Generally, the average six- or eight-point buck that falls far short of Boone and Crockett status might measure as low as 2 1/8 inches between the burrs, although 2 1/4 is more common. Oddly, a yearling spike buck might show a measurement of 2 1/2, but this is mainly because the corona and burr of a very young buck are still undeveloped. Let me summarize here: unless you're working with whitetail antlers of awesome trophy status, you really have only about a half-inch of burr-distance to play with, from about 2 1/4 to 2 3/4 inches.

Once the distance between the burrs has been established and both antlers have been at least temporarily fastened in place to the plaque or mounting base, you can begin experimenting with the inside spread. Of course, your primary goal here is to come up with a position that makes the antlers both look good and appear realistic. Here's a suggestion that will help you achieve both goals: Boone and Crocket scoring specifies that the inside spread should not exceed the length of the longest beam, and if it does, the length of that longest beam is substituted for the inside spread. In other words, if you take the time to measure the longest beam and then position the two antlers so that the inside spread is less than that, you're headed in the right direction. The median inside spread for recent B&C whitetail entries is very close to 19 1/2 inches, and the median length of the longest beam is 26 inches. This means that the average B&C deer has an inside spread that is 75 percent of the length of the longest beam. Of course, half the deer registered by Boone and Crockett are larger than this and the other half are smaller, so you still have to eyeball the rack until the positon seems right to you.

There is no online Boone and Crockett data for the distances between the tips of the antlers, because that measurement isn't used in the final score; it's just taken to help identify and characterize the rack. Even if we had the median of all the measurements, it would still be more important to position the two shed antlers so that the "basket shape" is approximated, with the tines arranged in such a way as to best grapple with another buck's antlers for a pushing contest.

For any wall mount, whether the antlers are loose sheds or have been cut from the buck's head as an intact rack with a portion of the original skull still attached, there can be a problem with the forward tilt of the finished rack. There are no set guidelines or recommended dimensions for this, but you certainly don't want the rack to seem to droop toward the floor. My personal opinion is that the tips of the main beams should be a couple of inches lower than the pedicles from which the antlers are attached to the skull. (Or, with shed antlers, where the butt-ends are located.) This enables the viewer to get a better look at the full sweep and curve of both main beams, and most of the tines will be in a near-vertical position.

Ideally, for a whitetail, the base that the antlers are mounted on should only be, at the most, less than half an inch wider than the width of the paired antlers at their base. If it is any wider than that, your antler

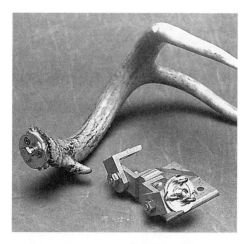

This adjustable system for mounting deer shed antlers first involves attaching a connector to the butt-end of each antler.

Once the connectors are attached, the antlers can be tightly fastened to the interlocking device. Inside spread, tip-to-tip distance, and overall tilt can be adjusted and then locked into place for mounting on a plaque or a polyurethane form.

mount will look as though someone had poked twigs into a bowling ball. Remember, a whitetail buck's head is basically flat between its antlers, and the antlers themselves grow out of the top edges of that "square" head. A smaller base will make the antlers appear larger. (The actual wood plaque to which the base will be attached will, of course, be considerably wider.)

Mechanical Devices for Positioning Shed Antlers

Mechanical devices such as the "Shed Connection" (available at most taxidermy supply houses or www.mckenziesp.com) create an artificial version of a skull plate on which shed antlers can be positioned on steel pegs and fastened in place with wood screws before being mounted. Once the butt-ends of the antlers are anchored to the interlocking system, you can adjust the inside spread, the tip-to-tip distance, and the tilt by loosening the mechanical parts and retightening them. Then, the entire ensemble (the antlers plus the interlocking system) can be placed on a plaque or even the mounting form of a full shoulder mount.

Do-It-Yourself Mounting of Shed Antlers

You'll need a plaque for wall-hanging and a smaller base that will substitute for the missing section of deer skull that would otherwise have held both antlers in the correct position. The base is attached to the plaque, and then the antlers are attached to these assembled parts. (Of course, you can make these yourself, although the commercially available kits are handsome and relatively inexpensive. To make your own base for whitetail and mule deer shed antlers, cut a circle about 4 inches in diameter from 1-inch-thick pine, and bevel the edges for covering— see Step 7 below.) To mount the antlers, follow these steps:

1. Attach the base to the plaque, preferably with counter-sunk wood screws.
2. Drill a $^1/4$-inch-diameter hole into the end of each antler to a depth of about 1 inch.
3. Cut a 5-inch length of 6-gauge wire and epoxy one end snugly into the drilled hole. Repeat for the other antler. (You can substitute $^3/16$-inch threaded rod for the wire. It's not as flexible as the wire, but the threading helps hold a steady position in the epoxy, and it's possible to actually bolt the loose end behind the plaque. Both the wire and rod can be found in most hardware stores. If you're really desperate or in a hurry, use a double strand of old coat-hanger wire, twisted together.
4. Drill two $^1/4$-inch holes in the mounting base where you want to attach the antlers, and continue all the way through to the back of the plaque. Use the preferred distance between burrs as your guide, but remember that you'll be drilling these holes for the *center* of each antler's base, so you'll need to add half the diameter of the antler on each side.
5. When the epoxy has hardened, poke the wires through the base and firmly attach the loose ends to the back of the plaque.
6. Adjust the antlers by moving and bending the wires until the correct positions are achieved.
7. The antlers can then be permanently and firmly shimmed into position using automotive body-repair compounds such as "Bondo-Glass." This material, or modeling clay, should also be used to smooth out the wood base so that it is rounded. The base then needs to be given an attractive covering; leather and velvet work best.

Antlers make for a dramatic display when starkly silhouetted against a window.

Mirror-Image Shed Antlers

I've heard about this method for viewing and displaying single shed antlers, but I never tried it myself until just recently. Much of the time, shed-hunters find only one antler from any given deer. We try hard, but either someone else finds the other antler, or the squirrels or porcupines do and proceed to chew it up. So there we are, holding one antler and trying so hard to imagine how the full rack would have looked that it almost gives us a headache. Well, here's a technique for seeing or even permanently mounting a single antler as a seeming "full rack." All you need is a mirror.

When you hold an antler near a mirror, you see two antlers and yourself. (Forget yourself for right now, OK? Maybe later you can come back alone.) If you step to one side and move closer to the mirror so you are looking at the original antler at about a 45-degree angle or more, you'll see it reflected as though it were a full rack. This works especially well if the butt-end of the shed antler is held within 1 1/4 inch of contacting the mirror. (Remember, the average burr-to-burr distance for most whitetails is about 2 1/2 inches.) If the original shed antler was the buck's left antler, then hold it as though the deer were facing to the left, or in the opposite direction for the right antler. By tipping the antler one way or another, you can also adjust the effective "inside spread" measurement.

Now, wouldn't this be an eye-catcher as a permanent mount? In fact, wouldn't this be a great way to mount several single antlers, all lined up along the bottom of the same rectangular mirror? This style of mounting a single shed antler would work especially well in a corner that, because of the layout of the room, doesn't let you easily stand in front of the mirror. Just don't do it with the bathroom mirror; you could hurt yourself some dark night.

A Basket of Shed Antlers

Not all shed antlers are suitable for mounting, especially when you don't have a matching pair. Most sheds are modestly sized spikes and fork-horns, although it makes sense that a disproportionate number of the larger antlers get found just because they're bigger and easier for the shed-hunter to find. Big or small, however, it seems a shame to store

A basket of antlers can keep some people occupied for hours. Kids and adults alike apparently receive satisfaction from rearranging antlers until their positions are "just right."

sheds in a cardboard box out in the garage where no one can see them. A good way to make them more accessible and easier to show off, even the small ones, is to pile them into a wicker basket. Keep the basket on the coffee table or a similar location where people, including you, can pick them up. This not only makes a handsome display, but most people, whether they've ever had a single thought about antlers, like to feel the heft and balance of a "sculpture" from nature.

MOUNTING FULL RACKS

A set of antlers can be considered to be a full rack when both of them are attached to at least a portion of the original skull. There's no question about what the correct positions of the antlers should be, because what you see is what the deer was actually wearing. The most common source of full racks is, of course, bucks or bulls killed by hunters, with the antlers mounted as a trophy representing the outcome of the hunt. But full racks are often found on deer that have died for unknown reasons in the woods, or have been hit by cars, and so on, and the Boone and Crockett Club allows the registration of such full racks if their score meets the minimum standards. What this could mean to you, if you happened to be at the right garage sale at the right time and found someone getting rid of old Uncle Fred's 1936 trophy, is that you could end up with several thousand dollars' worth of some deer's headbones. That's if the antlers are still connected to a piece of the original skull. If they aren't, you're still lucky, but now you're down to considerably less money.

A rack from a freshly killed deer shrinks slightly during the sixty-day waiting period required for official scoring. As the thin seam of cartilage at the centerline of the skull contracts, the inside spread is capable of decreasing by up to half an inch, and sometimes considerably more on larger deer and elk. Many taxidermists routinely place a wood stick between the tips of a deer's antlers to force the cartilage to stretch rather than letting the spread shrink, but this should not be done with potential Boone and Crockett qualifiers.

If you plan to have a deer-head mount done by a taxidermist, the entire hide and severed head should be left intact. The taxidermist will ultimately remove the hide and saw off the top portion of the skull, to which the antlers are attached. He or she will then attach the skull section and the antlers to a lifelike mounting form, and . . . well, let's not go into the full-fledged details of professional taxidermy here. Let's instead stay with just preparing the antlers for mounting.

Taxidermist Evelyn Maryanski of Franklinville, New York, begins the final saw cut to remove antlers from the skull of a 160-inch whitetail buck.

If you have your deer butchered by a professional venison processor and you want to keep the antlers, just tell him what you want. If you happen to be stopping by his shop on a slow day, the odds are good that he can remove them as an intact rack right on the spot. If not, make certain that you securely attach identification to those antlers; in fact, it might be wise to do that even before you take the deer to him. Most venison butchers have a special portable power saw that can cut down through a skull even faster than you can say, "Wow! So *that's* what brains look like!"

If you remove the full rack yourself, you'll have even more time to inspect the brains, whether you want to or not. It's an awkward job if you're not prepared with a work space, your hunting knife, a pair of pliers, and a really sharp carpenter's saw or hacksaw. The procedure of sawing is helped a lot if you first remove the deer hide from the area on the skull that you plan to remove. That's where you use the knife and pliers. There are then three different ways to make those saw-cuts, depending on the type of mount you want.

To fit antlers to a preformed plastic skull cap: Most commercially available skull cap kits are grooved to a depth of an inch or more to receive the portion of skull that holds the two antlers together. Take close notice of the position and shape of that groove, and plan your saw-cuts accordingly. Typically, you will make two angled cuts, one beginning an inch behind the antlers and the other beginning a couple of inches in front of the antlers, so as to cut a triangular wedge out the deer's head to which the antlers are both attached.

Once this wedge is freed from the carcass, any remaining hide and adhering brain and flesh must be removed. It's a good idea to sterilize the skull portion with boiling water or a diluted solution of laundry bleach. Once the antlers have been attached to the plastic cap, it can be covered with the fabric or leather contained in the kit according to the instructions provided.

To fit antlers to a homemade base: Only one saw cut is needed here. Begin right behind the antlers and saw directly toward the tops of the deer's eyes. It helps if you actually let the flat of the saw touch the burrs of both antlers and be guided by them. Continue sawing until you emerge at the surface again (a distance of about 4 inches) and the entire full rack can be lifted from the deer. Clean the attached portion of skull as described above.

You now have two options: attaching this circular skull cap directly to a plaque or attaching it to a raised platform that is then affixed to the plaque with counter-sunk screws coming in from the back. If you choose the second option, trace the skull cap's circular outline on 1-inch-thick wood and cut it slightly oversize so that you can round off the edges; this will be the platform. The advantage of this second option is that when you later cover the cap with velvet, leather, or perhaps copper sheeting, you can tuck the outside edges under this wood base and fasten them there, out of sight. You might need to fill in the shallow places with ordinary modeling clay before applying the cover.

To create a half-skull "European Mount": A European mount is perhaps the best alternative to an expensive, professionally done full-head-and-shoulder mount, and making it is far easier than you might think. It involves sawing from about 2 inches behind the antlers in the direction of the deer's nose, so that all the deer's upper teeth and lower jaw are left with the carcass. As potentially gruesome as this might sound, the finished product has a certain bestial beauty. By removing the lower jaw, you also remove the otherwise ugly, wide grin of bare teeth. Furthermore, this technique makes the antlers appear more impressive by effectively making the entire skull smaller than the actual head. This effect is particularly enhanced because the deer's wide ears are missing from the view that you'll have of the finished product.

This technique also exposes the brain cavity for easier removal of those interior tissues. The hard part involves removing all the flesh, brain, eyeballs, and other tissue that will be contained there. No, no, don't get the idea that you can place the half-skull and antlers on an anthill or on a barn wall so the insects can do your dirty work! Bad things will happen if you try that; if some dog doesn't drag your trophy away, or the squirrels don't start chewing on the antlers, it's for certain that within a day or so the flesh that you wanted the bugs to eat will be tougher than venison jerky, and even their maggots will go looking for something easier to chew. You might try to boil the skull in the kitchen to sterilize it and "cook" the adhering flesh off, but I sincerely doubt that you have a pot large enough to do that without the antlers getting in the way and preventing full submersion. Your best bet is to get a disposable aluminum roasting pan or an old galvanized washbasin to place on a grill over a campfire in your backyard. Then you can set up folding chairs and invite folks over for a head-cooking party. (Don't worry, they'll come.)

If you instead elect to do this cooking step in the kitchen against my advice, please be aware that all the water vapor from that boiling pot can peel the wallpaper right off the walls. Should this catastrophe happen, when your wife gets home just tell her that there was an earthquake while she was gone . . . and that you're cooking her a venison stew for supper. Quickly add carrots and onions and a *lot* of garlic and, if you have to, blame me.

The cooked flesh won't just fall off the skull; it has to be picked off. A nut-pick works very well here. The nasal chambers are amazingly complex, and as you work through the various layers of paper-thin bone that partition the many chambers within it, you'll gain additional insight into why deer have such a keen sense of smell. You would too, if you had a nose the size of your forearm.

Eventually the skull will be clean enough for you to progress to the "bleaching" stage. Using laundry bleach and an ordinary basting brush or paint brush, paint the skull—or, if you're able, submerge it in a water-bleach solution—to sterilize both it and any remaining particles of internal flesh. Don't worry if you bleach the antlers; you can always return them to natural color with a glossy wood stain.

Now you're finished, except for fastening the skull mount to the wall. This is no problem. Just place a hanger on the wall where you want the back of the deer's skull to be located. Then, with a drill, groove a small indentation on the inside of the skull where the holder will fit. A European-style mount looks good on an impressive oak panel, but you might prefer to just hang an empty picture frame around the antlers.

Detachable Antler Mounts for Elk, Caribou, and Moose

The huge antlers of trophy-size elk, caribou, and moose are best mounted using detachable connections for the convenience of handling and shipping. I suspect that more than once a big-antlered critter has been mounted with the antlers tightly fastened before the discovery is made that it won't fit through the door. Anyone who has ever built a canoe in their basement knows what I'm talking about. With a detachable mount installed, you can easily lift each antler separately off the head or skull-plate. Each attachment consists of a square steel bar embedded in the butt of the antler and a square steel sheath embedded in the pedicle of the skull. (Remember, the bony pedicle extends for an inch or three above the animal's skull—the length depends on the species—and is not a part of the antler.) They fit together like a hand in a glove.

The procedure for installing the attachments involves drilling a $1/4$-inch pilot hole from the inside of the brain cavity up through the pedicle and into the base of each antler. You then saw through each pedicle to free the antlers from the skull so that the right-size holes can be drilled to accommodate the bar and sheath. In the kit that I obtained from the Into the Wilderness Trading Company (www.bigantlers.com) in Wyoming, the bar is about $3/8$ inches square and 5 inches long; the hollow sheath into which the bar fits is $1/2$ inch square by 3 inches long. Once you know your measurements, you don't need detailed instructions; following the original pilot hole, you just drill the appropriately sized holes, epoxy both steel pieces firmly in place . . . and you're done.

Where this gets difficult is if you don't have access to the brain side of the skull in order to drill the pilot hole. In this case, you'll have to finagle the positioning of bar and sheath. Under these circumstances, it would be best not to epoxy the bar into place until you've had a chance to check the position of the antlers; that way, you can slip the steel bar out and bend it in a vise until you get the angle you want.

Then, epoxy the bar into the antler and prop the antler in the desired position until the epoxy has hardened. If you took good measurements of the inside spread and tip-to-tip spread while the rack was still on the deer, you'll be well prepared to achieve the correct position while the epoxy is still wet.

FAKING IT WITH ANTLERS

Antlers are naturally beautiful just the way they are, whether still attached to an old boss buck, the burrs all gnarly and stained brown and green from battles with other bucks and bushes, or as dry, old sheds whitened by a year or more of sunlight and moisture. If antlers that you've recently collected are a bit too fresh, or too chalky from exposure to the elements, they almost always can be improved by proper staining, oiling, polishing, and/or repairing. Reproduction of full trophy racks is now possible, and the results—the newly molded antlers—also need to be treated to obtain a more natural color than that of the vinyl compounds from which they are made.

Staining for Natural Coloration

A fresh antler is probably best left alone except when it's just plain dirty. After all, as we've seen elsewhere, whitetail bucks and other male deer often find ways to scent their antlers with their own urine . . . and that smell is one thing you *don't* want hanging over the fireplace. You can adequately clean an antler using just warm water and dish detergent. An old toothbrush (or your spouse's—just don't tell him or her) is good for removing the debris attached to the surface, but take it easy on the streaks and patches of dark coloration protected by the grooves in the burr; you don't want to remove all of this, because it contributes to the visual beauty of the antler.

Old shed antlers are sometimes discolored where they've been in contact with the moist forest floor, and here again the use of detergent will in most cases even up the usual white color. I've found from personal experience that a brownish wood stain diluted with paint thinner will very nicely imitate the natural pale yellow-brown of a fresh antler. So will a stain mixed with a glossy polyurethane. The main problem with this technique is that if you use too much stain, the antler will be too dark. Also note that the older an antler is, the more quickly it soaks up the stain, which can lead to blotching in some cases. It's best to begin with a solution that seems too weak to achieve the colors that you want and wait a half hour before checking the results; often, you'll find that it is sufficient to get what you had only hoped for. Another good thing about starting with an overly thinned solution is that it soaks into the porous structure of an antler, making the antler a bit more resistant to taking on too much color from subsequent coatings. Removing or lightening an excessive stain can be accomplished with ordinary laundry bleach, but this almost always takes you back to square one and, sometimes, the overall appearance of your next attempt is uneven or even blotchy.

Oiling and Polishing

Oiling an antler can add a gloss that makes it look fresher (and thus more valuable). Please understand that trying to make an old, white, chalky, shed antler look like something a 2 1/2-year-old buck shed last month is not only ill-advised—it even borders on the fraudulent, sort of like messing around with your car's odometer. Still, there's something basically satisfying about rubbing an old, dry antler with vegetable oil (or linseed oil) over several days until it just can't absorb any more. You rub off the excess liquid, wait for a few days, and then apply a stain. Or, begin with a water-based stain, perhaps one of your own concoction using paints and an acetone thinner, and then apply the oil after the stain has dried.

A fresh antler, whether recently shed or taken from a kill, can be polished to a degree that literally makes it glow like pure ivory. I've only seen this done once to an entire antler, and the effect was striking. The craftsman had ground off the outer $1/16$ inch of the naturally colored surface on most of the antler, graded it into the butt-end burr, and then polished the white surface with a rotary tool.

Antler Repair

(*Note:* The following detailed procedure for repairing broken antlers was kindly provided by Glen Conley of Whitetail Designer Systems, Inc., 866-849-9198.)

Broken antlers can be repaired with ordinary materials such as automotive body filler, copper wire, masking tape, and oil paints. To replace a lost antler tine, you first drill an oversized hole into the broken end of the antler and fill the hole with freshly mixed body filler. As soon as that is done, insert twisted 12-gauge copper wire deep into the hole and prop it in place until the filler becomes firm, usually within five to ten minutes.

Using ordinary masking tape, form a trough around the wire, approximating the desired length and shape. Fill the mold with body filler, allow it to harden just slightly, and then pull off the tape. Within

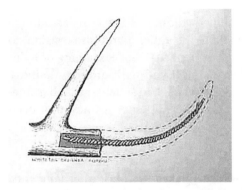

Broken antler tines can often be remolded with automotive body filler.

the next half-hour, while the filler is firm but not yet too hard, whittle it to match the basic shape you want. To avoid breaking off the tip, carve back toward where the thicker portion of the main beam would be. After the tine has hardened, sand it with garnet paper or emery cloth. Fill in any low spots and sand them smooth. Be careful when using this technique that you do not get the repaired area "too perfect," which is, unfortunately, easy to do. Be a little rough and create at least some of the irregularities that would be consistent with the rest of the antlers. This technique can also be used to lengthen a tine that is too short—or even to create an extra tine to give a rack a more balanced look.

Painting a repaired section to recreate natural colors can been done with artist's oil paints. Antler color shades and tints vary greatly, so get your eyeballs and mind in focus and ask yourself, "What colors do I see where?" With fresh brown antlers the natural color is often a mixture of burnt umber, yellow ochre (light), and Payne's gray "milked out" with titanium white and chrome yellow (medium hue). Hey, calm down—it's not as hard as it sounds. Mix a teeny bit of medium-hue chrome yellow with titanium white just to the point of being a slightly yellowish white. (The chrome yellow is a transparent oil paint. The use of it in the mix up front helps avoid that obvious "painted look.") Paint this onto the bare body filler after thinning it down with mineral spirits to the point that it just covers the section without the filler showing through. After doing that, add just enough light yellow ochre to the mix to produce an antler color. Eyeball the tips on the rest of the antlers and decide where to apply the horn color. Use a dry-brush technique: take a brush with a flat, stiff bristle, dip only the tip in the paint, and apply it in the desired areas with blotchy strokes. Clean the brush every two or three strokes. Adding some Payne's gray to the mix may help to achieve a more accurate coloration.

Next, take a drop of burnt umber and smear it out thinly on your palette. Use the same flat, hard-bristled brush and just barely tip it with the umber. Jab the tip of the brush onto the painted surface in a pattern consistent with the brown you see on the other tines. Clean the brush every two or three jabs. Once the umber is in place, use a soft, flat brush and lightly stroke the painted area to blend and smooth the paint. Keep the brush clean. Stroke with one side, turn it over, and clean the brush; this will help keep from turning the colors muddy.

You can see additional illustrations of these techniques online by going to http://whitetaildesignersystems.homestead.com.

Antler Reproductions

Over the past one hundred years, fewer than a couple hundred 200-inch typical whitetail racks have been registered by the Boone and Crockett Club. Considering the rarity of these high-end trophies, it's no wonder that antler mania is driving antler prices into the tens of thousands of dollars and even, in some cases, over the hump into the hundred-thousand-dollar ballpark. With prices like these, there has been an increasing demand for replica antlers, which are usually under $1,000 (though they can go for up to $5,000 if the rack is especially famous; for a sample selection with prices, check out www.deergear.com). Even that may seem high to you, but so far, no one has developed a system that can reproduce large quantities of high-quality replica antlers at low cost. Single antlers are relatively easy to mold, but the process for trophy racks attached to the original skull is highly labor-intensive and requires a certain degree of artistic skill and a whole bagful of patience.

Below is one procedure for reproducing antlers. It is only a very brief outline of the procedure that was supplied to me by Larry Blomquist, who actually developed some of the techniques used here. Blomquist is also the editor of the taxidermy magazine *Breakthrough*, where the procedure originally appeared in full detail. It's called the cradle method, and the mold in it can be used several times. For this method to work correctly, the original pair of antlers will need to be on a skull cap.

1. A wood platform is installed inside the brain cavity so that the entire rack can be fastened to a flat board for convenience of handling, and the inner eye sockets are closed off with modeling clay. A dam, also made of clay, is built around the skull on the flat board to prevent molding materials from escaping during the procedure.

2. Two different materials are used to make the mold. The first is a pourable silicone rubber material that is painted on the antlers and skull and allowed to dry. An additional coat (or coats) is frequently needed.

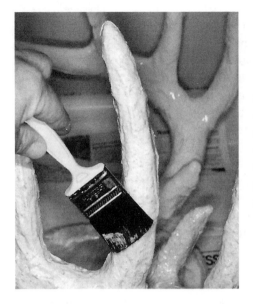

Creating a mold for casting replicas of antlers involves repeated applications of two different silica rubber materials. When cured, the pliable coating can be removed and becomes the new mold.

3. A coating of the thicker silicone rubber material is spread over the outside of the soft mold to hold everything in place. It can be applied with disposable paint stirrers. This second coating dries into a more rigid structure that supports the weaker, inner surface. Again, you'll probably need additional coats, which should this time be smoothed with acetone.

4. Build a wood support structure along the centerline of the skull. It must include a cross-brace that supports both antlers. The structure will prop up the mold when the antlers are later

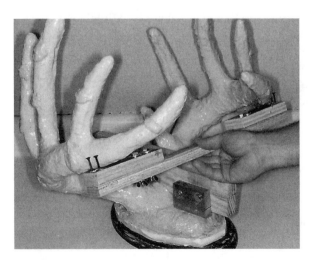

Once removed, the pliable mold will require external support before it can be coated with a fiberglass putty that hardens into a supporting "cradle."

removed. (A good structure is far more complicated than I can do justice to here. In the photos, it has been screwed into place.)

5. Using an automotive fiberglass body putty such as Bondo-Glass, cover only the outer portions of the skull and antlers. The inside surfaces of the rubber mold (where the inside spread would be measured in scoring) should still be exposed as they were after Step 3. Allow the putty to harden; it will later form a supportive "cradle" for the outer, rounded surface of the antlers.

6. The wood supports and the two fiberglass cradles can now be removed. (Are you beginning to understand why replica antlers cost so much?) This fully exposes the soft, flexible silicone rubber molds.

7. Using a razor, cut seams in the rubber mold along surfaces that will be hidden from a front view. With an uncomplicated typical whitetail rack, a single cut two-thirds the length of the main beam is usually enough to allow removal of the entire antler on each side of the rack. The tines will usually pull out of the soft mold with no additional cuts needed.

8. Reassemble the rubber mold inside the Bondo-Glass cradle, making sure all the seams that you cut are realigned, and then bind it and the cradle securely together in several locations with masking tape.

9. Turn the assembly upside-down, held up by a wood support, revealing the hollow interior. Mix casting plastic (available in many art and hobby stores) and pour it very slowly first into one antler, then into the other; this alternation helps to avoid trapping bubbles in the tines. Rock the mold slowly to release any bubbles. Also, poke a stick or plastic straw down into the antler, especially around the burr region; this will force the liquid into the crevasses of the burr. Work fast, because the casting plastic becomes firm within minutes, although it requires about four hours to fully harden.

10. Remove the replica antlers the same way you earlier removed the actual antlers. Be careful: the plastic isn't as strong as real antlers. The seams can be scraped clean with a dull knife. With care and maybe a bit of repair, the mold can be used multiple times.

11. Apply stains and other substances to the reproduction as described earlier in this chapter.

Taxidermist Bill Yox of Brockport, New York, holds a rack he replicated from a non-typical whitetail buck that was illegally taken in Ohio in 1975. The original antlers are owned by the Ohio Department of Natural Resources and were scored at 256 ⁵/8 inches.

THE RISKS OF DISPLAYING ANTLERS

If you didn't already know how difficult it is to replicate antlers, you now have a better understanding of why even phony antlers made with thirty dollars' worth of silicone rubber and a casting plastic can sell for at least twenty times more than that. Replicas of top Boone and Crockett racks easily sell for several thousands of dollars. Replica antlers are so often so convincing that they could be (and have been) sold as counterfeits for top dollar. (To tell if a rack is real or not, heat the point of a pin or needle with a match and then immediately try to stick it into the antler. If the pin sticks, the antler is a phony.) Real antlers are obviously worth much more than replicas . . . but we already covered that in Chapter 2.

Give the following some serious thought: Would you leave a coat rack in your house with thousands of dollars' worth of fifty-dollar bills taped to it like leaves on a tree and then go away on vacation? Probably

The remarkable buck from which these antlers were replicated was a 1996 Iowa kill by bowhunter Sam Collora. It was recorded by the Pope and Young Club as the highest gross score for a typical whitetail taken by an archer. Replication was done by Bryan Umbanhowar and the mounting with the original cape was done by taxidermist Gary Bowen.

not, but the equivalent happens all the time with antlers. There's a committed trophy hunter who lives a few miles away from me whose mounted antlers are worth more than his house. He's nervous about the possibility of theft and told me to not tell anybody who he is or where he lives. His trophy antlers are on display, but hardly anyone but him ever sees them. Another man I know has antlers in his barn worth roughly $50,000—and much more if he sold them individually online. This fellow wanted to increase the homeowner's insurance on his barn to include those antlers on his policy. The insurance agent just chuckled at the idea that "deer horns" might be worth anything at all. But the owner told him to look up antlers on eBay, so he did . . . and came back a few days later to give the owner what he'd requested.

These days, when a lucky hunter takes a respectable trophy head to the taxidermist, the taxidermist often doesn't bother to ask for a down payment. That's because the antlers can be worth considerably more than what the deposit would have been, and if the hunter later forfeits the mount because he can't or won't pay what he owes, the taxidermist comes out ahead. The demand for antlers is definitely high. Knowing this, and keeping in mind what can happen to quality antlers, be careful about where and how you display them.

7

CARVING
THE NEW IVORY

Even when held tightly, an antler almost always gives the impression of motion; it's like a frozen flame, or a grasping hand. The fact that it's made out of hard bone only adds to the feeling of aggressive force that it can project. When you're in an unfamiliar place, an unexpected glimpse of antler can actually startle you, as though the sharp tines were exclamation points indicating a sudden threat. With that as a starting point, it's no wonder antler carving has arisen as an art form! Add the recent growth of general interest in all deer species—as well as the dramatic growth of the actual whitetail deer population—and you can easily understand why something had to "break out" here.

ONE REASON THAT THE POPULARITY
OF ANTLER CARVING HAS INCREASED

Humans have been carving ever since there have been humans; in fact, one of the criteria that anthropologists use for determining whether the site of an archeological dig belonged to *Homo sapiens* instead of our precursors is whether some of the local stones and bones have been carved into tools. Widespread trade based on ivory tusks was one of the main reasons that human civilization spread throughout the northern hemisphere. In fact, fossilized mammoth tusks—and, to a lesser extent, mastodon tusks—are still important sources of ivory for hobbyist carvers. In Siberia, for example, there are believed to be literally thousands of mammoth tusks yet to be found, and an active market has grown up around mining this "new" source of ivory. There is also a vast supply of mammoth ivory in northern Canada—more than museums can handle worldwide—so the government (which usually claims the rights to prehistoric finds) has released the ivory for use by carvers as a substitute for modern-day elephant tusks.

Ivory also comes from the modern-day hippopotamus, walrus, and sperm whale. Still, most ivory originates in African elephant tusks. Whereas antlers are bone, elephant tusks are just overgrown teeth. Teeth in any mammal grow slowly from the roots; antlers are bones that grow rapidly only at the tips. Another difference: ivory has no system of blood vessels, and consequently is more dense and nonporous. The importation of elephant ivory to the United States is rigidly controlled and generally prohibited—one of the policies that is intended to curtail the poaching of elephants in Africa. Ironically, the curtailment has worked so well that in some areas of Africa the elephant population has grown out of control, like our American deer population! This has led to government-organized hunts in agricultural regions, and the resulting ivory is stockpiled by the governments for periodic auction. Nonetheless, the majority of elephant ivory that is available to hobbyist carvers in the United States usually comes from private owners who acquired their tusks in the 1960s and 1970s, before the import restrictions went into effect. This is called "estate ivory."

As you might imagine, with all the restraints and limitations on the American ivory trade, elephant ivory is very expensive. It's probably the best of all the carving mediums, due to its velvety color and luster (the result of a microscopic grain structure that changes as light hits it, somewhat like opals). But you pay through the nose for those qualities! For example, two pre-cut slabs of ivory such as you might want as decorative knife handles, each sized $1/8$ inch thick by $1\,1/2$ inches wide by $4\,1/2$ inches long, would cost you about $60. A small wafer cut as a cross-section from a small tusk, $1/8$ inch thick with a $2\,3/4$-inch diameter, goes for $22. Small bits and pieces suitable only for jewelry items and inlays are ordinarily priced from $20 to $80 per pound.

Compare these relatively high ivory prices to the typically low prices for whole, full-size craft antlers that you can make into just about anything. Obviously, deer antler is the better bargain for the hobbyist carver—and not a bad deal for the professional artist, too. At the same time that the availability of elephant ivory was being restricted in the 1980s, the whitetail deer population in North America began to swell, and by the twenty-first century, there were probably more deer than had ever lived at any one time. That meant more antlers available to collectors and carvers. Eventually it may come to pass that the elephant herds of Africa will become so large that the United States and other western countries will relax their importation restrictions and permit a renewed flow of ivory to collectors and carvers. Until that happens, antlers will continue to be the number one medium for that kind of carving.

Antler carver Jack Brown of Wellsville, New York, comes face-to-face with the artistic possibilities presented to him by a whitetail rack.

ANTLER CARVING AND THE INTERNET

What's really turned up the flame under carving is the exposure that the Internet has given it, especially eBay and similar sites, where, as I've said, at least a thousand antler-related items are being auctioned. (Go ahead . . . go ahead and check it out!) Antlers really are the "new ivory," and as the availability of ivory has declined, the market has shifted in the direction of antler art. Good antler carving is done so skillfully that "art" is the category it most accurately fits in. Collectors are gathering, even hovering, around antler carvers, wanting to be first to buy from the artists whose names will be well-known tomorrow or ten years from now. New names are appearing regularly, artists whose works might demand much bigger dollars in resale as time goes by.

Jack Brown, the "Bonecarver" of eBay fame, comes to mind. (Check out his website at www.bonecarver.com.) I recently visited him a couple of times in Wellsville, New York, to learn more about what the carving business and the art itself are all about. Brown's store, "Stones 'n Bones," right across the street from the post office, is one of the most interesting places I've ever been. There are antler carvings and other artifacts everywhere you look: in display cases, on the walls, suspended from the ceiling . . . and yes, some stuff is on the floor. No two items are alike, and that also seems to apply to the customers and gawkers who are constantly coming in the front door. While I was there, a nun came in to have a piece of antler affixed to the handle of her cane. There were a few tourists who wanted to buy something, anything, just so they could go back home to tell the story about how they'd discovered a store that "you'd never believe unless you saw it yourself!" A fellow stopped in with a cardboard box full of whitetail antlers for Jack to use in making a chandelier for him. A couple of Amish men brought in some antler sheds that they'd found. A teenage girl purchased some jewelry inlaid with antler. A married couple came in to discuss the terms for commissioning a carving from Jack. And so on.

When he wasn't dealing with all this or answering my questions about antler carving, Jack would go to his computer to check the online bidding on a couple of his items. The first year that Jack sold something on eBay (2001), he was just hoping to pick up a little money for Christmas gifts for wife Melanie and their six kids. The first items sold so quickly that Internet auctioning soon became his primary source of income, and the store is now his warehouse for items to be auctioned in the future . . . unless they get sold before that time comes. Internet sell-

Shedhunter, a Labrador retriever owned by Jack Brown, does double duty as a guard dog for Jack's antlercraft store.

*"Dueling Dragons,"
a commissioned
artwork, was carved
by Jack Brown from
two shed antlers
provided by Dean
Ziegler for the 2004
"Deerassic Classic"
fund-raiser.*

ing can be tricky, though, and there's apparently an art to it. As Jack explained, "You need a good description directed at what people want, and you need to have items constantly coming up to the deadline and other items being sold. There's a lot of time that goes into online selling, and if you maintain high quality and a good flow, you'll develop a nice following."

In 2004, Jack was commissioned by the National Whitetail Deer Education Foundation to carve two shed antlers into "Dueling Dragons" that were raffled for several thousand dollars, all for the benefit of the education center at Deerassic Park, near Cambridge, Ohio. Ordinarily, Jack specializes in carving the heads of screaming eagles from the butt ends of thick antlers, posing them in such a way that the flaring tines of the antler resemble the eagle's wings. He often combines that motif with a separate carving of the clenched talons of the avian predator, and the effect is striking. I watched him one afternoon as he carved an eagle. He first spent several minutes just looking at the original antler, a hefty whitetail with four points on it. (The coronet had been sliced off earlier for use as a medallion.) Jack held the antler in several positions and then reached for a rotary tool to lightly trim off the heavy burr at the antler's base. This provided him with a trimmed, white, ivorylike surface on which he could sketch with a pencil the preliminary profile of an open-mouthed eagle. He then marked the opposite side of that profile as the first step toward creating a three-dimensional view. I could see that he had planned ahead to include two of the antler's "holes" (see "Antler Hardness" on the next page), one an artery, the other a vein, as the nostrils in the eagle's beak. That third dimension is where true antler art is conceived and made. Carving "in the round," so that an object can be viewed from any angle and still make sense, offers a beguiling mixture of art and artisanship and is where carving crosses the line from craft projects into sculpture. This eagle turned out to be a work of art that went for auction on eBay, and some other person owns it now.

ANTLER HARDNESS

Antlers are bones, and that should probably be the end of the subject. But somehow I just can't stop there. Antlers are actually "bony," not exactly the same as hollow, marrow-filled bones, but still composed primarily of calcium hydroxyapatite (the same thing as the ordinary calcium supplement that you might be taking at breakfast), with smaller amounts of calcium carbonate (also used as ordinary chalk), calcium fluoride (a naturally occurring mineral used in toothpaste to prevent cavities), and magnesium phosphate (which, in addition to a thousand other uses, can be used to keep the salt in your shaker from forming lumps and . . . um, as a laxative). About a third of the remaining substances in antlers is ossein, which is a hard gelatin that is commonly extracted from cow bones to put the "gloss" into photographic prints— even now, in the twenty-first century. No kidding. I looked it up, and when I did that, I also found a recipe from 1875 for making edible antler jelly by boiling antler chips to extract the gelatin. This is not a joke. You'll find the recipe at the end of this chapter.

The best part of an antler for carving is the hard outer surface, where the structure is most uniformly solid. Yes, antlers are bones, but they don't contain the typically hollow core of spongy, fat-filled marrow the way ordinary animal bones do. Still, if you saw through an antler so that its slightly porous center is revealed, you'll usually see a couple of very small holes; these mark the locations of the veins and arteries that nourished the growing antler when it was still in velvet. In fact, if a growing antler happens to be cut when it's still in velvet, as occurs when one is surgically removed for use in health-food supplements, blood can spurt several yards unless the wound is staunched. What this means to the antler carver is that no antler is completely solid all the way through. Part of the art of antler carving is being able to incorporate this flaw into the beauty of the design.

The antlers of deer, elk, and caribou have a hard, dense layer surrounding a softer, less dense core, and if you look even more closely at that cross-section you've cut, you'll also find a scattering of porosity. The structure of these antlers is tubular, with the strength in the outer shell, so the inner part can be supported by a lighter, honeycombed structure that can absorb and diffuse the sustained stresses of close-contact pushing and twisting. Sculptor Shane Wilson, who specializes in creating large, complex scenes on moose antlers, explains that the porosity in the interior, or "web," of moose antler is relatively low so that it can act as a single layer, able to flex on impact. Bull moose charge from distances of several yards and slam head-on into each other. If the webbing of moose antlers was as porous as tubular antlers, it would be prone to splitting and breakage.

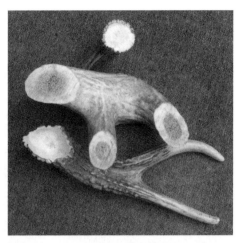

Sawed cross-sections of antlers reveal an inner core of porosity left by the blood vessels of the growing velvet antler. The artist-carver needs to accommodate this region in the design of most figures.

The hardness of antler material is not the only thing different for each of the species; the location of the core porosity also varies. Whitetail deer antlers contain the highest percentage of workable material for carving. (The mule deer is probably the same as the whitetail, but no one I spoke to could say that for certain.) In general, the hardness and density of the outer surface on a whitetail antler increase the closer you are to the ends of the tines or the basal (butt) ends. Even within a species, though, hardness can vary, probably as a result of diet and the mineral content of the available forage.

The different species' antlers are ranked as follows, in order from hardest to softest:

1. Whitetail Deer
2. Mule Deer
3. Moose
4. Elk
5. Caribou

The best antlers for carving vary depending on what you want to do with them. Yes, whitetail deer (and mule deer) antlers contain a higher percentage of dense material for carving, but they're generally

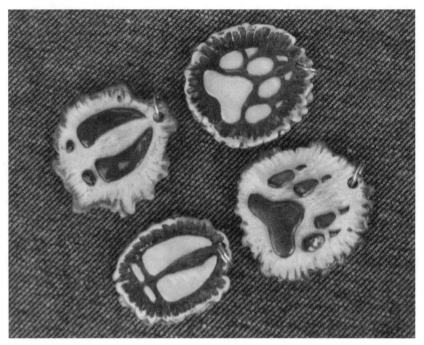

Medallions can be sliced from the butt-end of an antler, with the knurled fringe of the coronet included in the widest ones. The sawed surface can be stained or colored with indelible ink so that a design can be carved using a rotary tool.

significantly smaller than the antlers of elk, caribou, and moose. Further, as mentioned above, the truly dense material on a whitetail antler is located in the tines and nearest the surface of the main beams, which limits most carvers to small items such as knife handles and buttons or to sculptured shapes such as dragons or eagles that follow the external curves of the original antler. Even then, the carving is best done in low relief on the surface layer as much as possible to avoid exposing the interior. The wide, palmated antlers of moose, on the other hand, have a relatively dense consistency throughout that tolerates deep carving.

As we've seen, antlers remain "alive" long after the velvet is discarded and even up to the time when they are shed. They're actually in a sort of suspended animation, similar to an elephant's ivory tusks—which, although they are teeth instead of bones, are also alive. Scientists used to think that antlers "died" during the loss of the velvet covering, while they were still on the deer's head, but recent tests have proven that a very slow-but-sure flow of blood continues to nourish the antler and prevent it from becoming brittle. This is why freshly shed antlers are free of the "chalky" texture of old sheds. Continued exposure of shed antlers to sunlight will bleach them and cause micro-cracking on and under the surface; exposure to changing temperatures on wet ground in colder climates can cause a leaching of calcium and phosphorous that weakens the original bone structure and creates that chalky feel. By oiling as described in Chapter 6, old, dry antlers can be made to look and carve almost like fresh sheds.

WHERE TO GET ANTLERS FOR CARVING

Several of the antler carvers and antler artisans that I interviewed for this book were not hunters and never had been. A few of them were shed-hunters who knew their way around the woods, but a goodly number of carvers and artisans had obtained their antlers by other methods. Here's a listing of the more common sources of antlers.

Roadkills

Gruesome as it might seem, one of the more opportunistic means of acquiring antlers is by sawing them off the occasional roadkill. In most parts of the United States, only about one out of five roadkilled deer will be an antlered buck . . . and by the next day, it will still be a dead buck, but it won't still be antlered if someone else has beaten you to it. Any hacksaw or carpenter's saw will do the job in less than two minutes; just be sure to saw the antlers down under the flared corona where the antler attaches to the skull. Now, in some states it's illegal to remove any part of a roadkilled deer that wasn't taken by a licensed hunter. That includes the venison and even the tail (which many trout fisherman might want in order to tie "streamer" lures). Sometimes the driver of the car that killed the deer can get a special permit by calling the police. So, check with your state's Department of Conservation—and keep a saw in your car.

Antique Stores

You can walk into just about any antique store these days to ask for antlers, and the newly enlightened people there won't look at you as though you're some hick screwball. Instead, they'll even know which aisle to send you to. The popularity of antlers has spread way beyond hunters, carvers, and artisans, and this has driven the prices up even in the antique market. Often the antlers you'll find in such a store will be on a deer's head that was mounted so many years ago that it looks downright ugly, but that's why it's still in the store. Nobody else dared to take it home. However, you can easily take the antlers off the mount just by making a couple of small cuts in the hide between the antlers to open up the seam. I guarantee you that the antlers will only be attached to a very small piece of skull, which will be fastened by wood screws to the mounting form. If this task takes more than five minutes of your time, you should forget those plans to become a brain surgeon.

Garage and Household Sales

There are more mounted deer, moose, elk, and caribou heads to be found in suburbia than you might have imagined. Those "summer sales" can produce a lot more antlers than going shed-hunting in the woods. Hunters enthusiastically get trophy heads mounted—and I respect that inclination—but after several years and maybe one new wife or two, the trophy winds up in the garage or attic. Most people who put on a sale wouldn't even bother to put a trophy on display, thinking that if they don't want it, nobody else would either. So, it doesn't hurt to ask the big question: "Got antlers?" Sometimes, if the husband isn't home to object, the wife may "find" antlers for you right over the fireplace!

Classified Advertisements

Using advertising to locate antlers betrays your desire to own them, which bumps the price up. Still, if you get replies, it's often worth your time to go take a look at them. If you're not sure about the price, take another look at the charts in Chapter 2: you conceivably could find a set of antlers worth thousands of dollars. You can often barter for smaller craft antlers, and your best offer will probably be something like the promise of a knife handle made from the very same antlers to which the guy still has as an attachment.

Venison Processors

The people who butcher deer into venison often throw the smaller antlers away. Little "spike" and "fork horn" antlers are ideal for machining into knife, fork, and spoon handles, drawer handles, buttons, and gun racks. They also provide you with a chance to practice your carving skills before starting on larger trophy antlers.

Online Suppliers

If all else fails, you can buy antler materials at online sites such as eBay and half.com. Although I've placed these suppliers here at the end of this list, this could be the best place to start if you're a total amateur and don't yet really know what this antlercraft thing is all about. As a carver, you should be looking for "craft antlers." Once you know what you want to do with antlers, you can be fairly certain of getting just what you want, such as (for example) five pounds of antler tines for utensil handles, or an entire thirty-pound elk shed antler, or a full, plaque-mounted whitetail rack with an estimated Boone and Crockett score. You'll also find the artistic products of carvers and artisans being sold online, priced at levels that reveal the high value of antler art.

ANTLER SCRIMSHAW

"Scrimshaw" as a word originally described the detailed scratchings that seamen made on the teeth and sometimes portions of the jawbones of sperm whales in the 1800s. Whaling ships spent long months at sea, and bored sailors spent some of their spare time creating these artifacts, which usually didn't qualify as art in the truest sense of the word but were worth at least a couple pints of ale in the next port. Small knives and nails—the only tools available—were used to scratch the teeth and bone, and soot from the whale-oil lamps was used to fill in and high-

Antler scrimshaw is often combined with cow horn scrimshaw, as with this antler rack for a powder horn created by Tim Ferrie of Russell, Pennsylvania.

light the markings. An entire art-culture has since built up around this colorful past, and today, some of these inscribed teeth are worth a whale of a lot of money.

Running parallel to this nautical tradition was the similar practice of inscribing and decorating the cow horns that were used as powder horns for muzzle-loading rifles. The horns of cattle don't shed every year the way antlers do, and before the development of the percussion rifle, there was a growing need for muskets in the New World and, later, the Wild West. Consequently, cow horns increased in value and were treated with more respect as a medium for decoration. Today, the primitive culture of the "mountain men" is being kept alive and well, and powder-horn scrimshaw is still widely practiced on cow horns. Scrimshawing (actually, the proper word here is "scrimshanding") has also survived in the engraving of soft metals such as copper, silver, and brass, but that's a different subject.

As far as whole antlers are concerned, there never has been much interest in actually doing scrimshaw. Even in ancient times, antlers were used as a raw material for the carving of small objects, but antler scrimshaw never quite caught on. The main reason for that is probably that antlers are brown instead of ivory-white, plus there's not much flat surface area on which to scratch pictures (except on moose antlers). There's also the problem of what to do with all that burr at the base and those odd little bumps here and there on the main beam. Here's my answer to that: be a true artist and work with what you have. Please keep reading!

There are at least two ways to make fresh antler look like ivory. The first is chemical whitening, which can be accomplished with ordinary household bleach. You daub the liquid on the antler a few times over a couple of days (in an open area, to avoid the fumes) and then rinse off the residue with fresh water. The second way involves sanding the brown surface away with coarse, then medium, and finally fine-grade sandpaper. Regardless of which whitening method you use, the antler is then polished with a buffing machine or with a series of progressively finer polishing substances such as steel wool and jeweler's rouge. The resulting product will look amazingly like pure ivory and will be in excellent condition for scrimshanding. I have seen this done in such a way that the bottom few inches of the antler—the butt-end—were left with the original brown coloration and rough burr, and it seemed as though a gleaming ivory antler had sprouted from the base with striking effect. Remember: if the surface of a carved item doesn't display some of the original antler's surface, you might just as well have carved

The surface of every antler is different from all the others in the way the burr, spikes, pearls, and coronet are placed.

it out of a cow bone. Unlike elephant ivory, which is valued for a pure, creamy color that serves well for scrimshaw and detailed carvings, authentic antler can't be recognized unless it displays the burr or other characteristic colors and surface textures.

One alternative to the classic scrimshaw method is to just use a fine-tipped pen with indelible ink (or a wood-burner pen) to carefully draw a design directly on the whitened antler. This isn't really carving—it's more like giving the antler a tattoo. The possibilities are limitless: A geometric pattern? A neatly written family genealogy utilizing the antler tines as branches? Perhaps a detailed account of how the antler was acquired? If you're more inclined to use scrimshaw for outdoor scenes and other images, you can draw on the polished antler with a lead pencil and then later erase those markings when you're done.

An antler can be carved and then polished to a white, ivorylike appearance.
Compare Jack Brown's carved antler to a similar one still in original condition.

Complex scenes can be transferred to the antler with carbon paper; all you have to do is tape the paper and then the desired image to the antler, where you can then trace the outline that you want to transfer.

EQUIPMENT FOR ANTLER CARVING

It's easy to get started in antler carving as a hobby. The basic equipment and tools are easy to get and reasonably priced, and you can learn the rudimentary techniques within a single day. What's the catch? Well, the time it takes to be a true master carver could be a lifetime, and . . . um, to get even better would take longer.

Nonetheless, the development of flexible-shaft rotary cutting tools (chiefly the Dremel and the Foredom) have made antler carving both more accessible and artistically possible for the amateur and the professional. These tools can be made to work like dentists' drills, and with a rotation speed of up to 35,000 rpm and a wide assortment of accessory cutters and bits, you can pull off just about every kind of carving, engraving, shaping, hollowing, grooving, sanding, grinding, and polishing you'd ever want to do on an antler. Rotary tools were developed and are marketed mostly for home carpentry and other do-it-yourself tasks, which means you can usually find them at reasonable prices in local hardware stores. No rocket science or sky-high prices here!

The Foredom rotary tools are the more powerful of the two types, capable of handling larger burrs, and they are best suited, for example, for whacking a moose antler down to workable size. The Dremel models are smaller and less expensive and can be used more effectively for the finer, close-up work. Now, I don't own either of these tools (yet!)

Flexible-shaft rotary cutting tools are essential for antler carving and are relatively inexpensive.

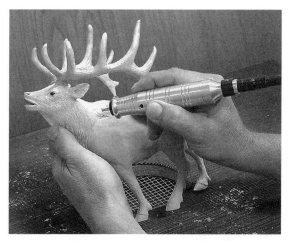

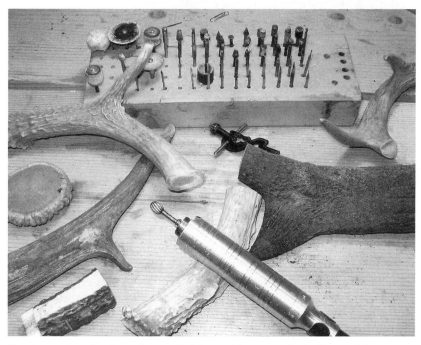

Foredom rotary tools can be applied in a wide range of grinding, cutting, sanding, and polishing jobs.

and am basing my comments here on the experiences of established antler carvers who seem to know what they're talking about. I'm a writer, not an artist.

Both brands of rotary grinders can be purchased with a range of accessories as complete kits at prices considerably lower than if you'd bought them one by one. A flexible shaft is included in some kits; for antler carvers, this is a near-necessity. If you're a tool junkie, you'll love all the options for accessories and cutters. There are more than 150 different sizes and shapes of drills, cutters, saws, diamond and carbide wheels, routers, grinding stones and grinding wheels, sanders, brushes, buffers, and polishers. You can see how antler carving could become such a strong addiction that you'd want to hurry through supper just to get to the workbench sooner.

Still, most carvers only need a few accessories. I asked Paul Blum, who is an online representative for the Dremel Company and is himself a carver, what he recommends for the sort of dragons-and-eagles antler art that Jack Brown produces. I wanted to know what the ideal progression of optional accessory types and sizes might be for the whittling of an antler, starting from scratch. Here's his advice:

- For the initial step of stock removal and basic shaping: structured-tooth tungsten/carbide cutters such as the $1/4$-inch cone, $5/16$-inch sphere and cylinder, and $3/4$-inch flat cylinder
- For the rough carving and shape formation: high-speed cutters such as the $3/32$-inch sphere, $5/16$-inch cone, and $5/64$-inch cylinder
- For the detailed carving and final shaping: engraving cutters such as the $1/16$-inch sphere and $1/32$-inch cylinder, and diamond-wheel points such as the $17/64$-inch saucer-disk, $5/64$-inch cone, and $3/32$-inch sphere
- For light touch-up sanding: sanding bands (120 grit) and finishing abrasive buffs
- For final polishing: polishing accessories such as the #414 disk, #422 cone, #423 disk/pad, #429 disk, and polishing wheel #520, which is a cylinder

For a different perspective, the following list of suggested equipment for an antler-carving seminar at Red Deer College in western Canada was provided by Yukon artist Shane Wilson:

- Dremel flexible-shaft grinder with with $1/8$-, $3/32$-, and $1/16$-inch collets
- Optional Foredom S-series flexible-shaft grinder with $1/8$-inch collets

- Assorted burrs with round and square tips
- Cloth polishing wheels
- Brown stone cone (or equivalent)
- White Tripoli polishing compound
- Safety gear: eye protection, hearing protection, one bike glove for the hand using the tool, one mesh or Kevlar glove for the hand holding the antler, and a leather apron

WHERE TO START?

So there you sit, an antler in one hand and a rotary tool in the other. Once you begin the process of cutting and drilling that antler, you can't erase any mistakes that you might make. There's no going back to square one unless you have more antlers than you know what to do with, which, of course, you don't and never will . . . ever. If you've just set up a new rotary tool and you just can't resist the urge to start carving *something*, practice first on stew bones, hardwood (such as a baseball bat), or even certain plastic toys. It helps if you have something

The beginner antler carver is advised to practice first with "bas-relief" sculptures in which the figures project just a short distance from a flat surface. These two were carved by Jack Brown.

already in three dimensions to copy, and again here's where you might want to raid some little kid's toys for prototypes.

When you do finally build up the courage to try carving a real antler, try to have a definite idea in mind about what it is that you want the figure to look like. Draw a picture beforehand. Consider also the positions of the tines on the antler: are there ways that you might make them into wings or legs? Should you cut the tips of any of them so that your figure might become free-standing? Once you're finished with this first effort, date and sign it, and then go on to your next attempt. It might be a bit soon to register on eBay as a seller of antler carvings, but you're headed in the right direction!

"EAT YOUR ANTLER DUST . . . SERIOUSLY"

By the time you've sawed, drilled, carved, and sanded a few antlers, you'll have produced a thick layer of antler dust and assorted shavings on your worktable. Disposal is no problem: you actually can eat your antler dust—if you cook it right! Some people still believe that dry antler dust is an aphrodisiac, but the male carvers and artisans that I interviewed for this book—men who machine antlers on a daily basis—told me that the stuff doesn't do *anything* for them. It's the velvet antler that contains the different growth hormones and steroids that conceivably could have an the desired effect, as explained in Chapter 5.

Sorry, guys, but probably the only thing that dry antler dust is good for is making gelatin, the cow version of which is the main ingredient in Knox Gelatin and is used along with sugar and colored food dyes in Jell-O. For several centuries, until the late 1800s, ordinary deer antler was the main source of gelatin for making fruit jellies. The only other source, isinglass, was the air bladder of the sturgeon. (Now, there's something you'd never have figured out using just your intuition!) The "Hartshorn Jelly" recipe that follows was named after the "hart," which was then the name for the European red deer. We don't have those in America except in zoos and on some velvet deer farms, so this recipe surely refers to the whitetail deer.

From *The Young Housewive's Counsellor and Friend: Containing Directions in Every Department of Houskeeping, Including the Duties of Wife and Mother*, by Mrs. Mary Mason (1875)
Rasp half a pound of hartshorn and boil it in three quarts of water. Then cover the saucepan closely and boil the hartshorn till wholly dissolved and reduced to two-thirds. Flavor and prepare as shown below.

Pare off the yellow rinds of four lemons, cut them into narrow strips, break into small pieces two long sticks of cinnamon; put these into a large bowl with one pound of sugar, and add the juice of the lemons, with the white of one egg, and a pint of white wine. Now add the gelatin to the contents of the bowl as soon as it is cool. Mix the whole well; pour it into a porcelain kettle, boil it fifteen minutes, and then pass it through a jelly-bag. On no account press the bag.

8

ANTLER FABRICATION
GONE WILD

COMMERCIAL ANTLERCRAFT

Some of the most interesting stores in America are located in rural towns near ski resorts. It's in places like these that an abundance of money, an outdoor sports culture, and a reasonably enlightened clientele with a sense of adventure can come together to foster creativity on both sides of the sales counter. One such town is Ellicottville, which is in the western end of New York State and is home to not just one but two ski resorts. That's where I first found "Gone Wild Creations," a 2,000-square-foot antler-furniture workshop. Antlers of every kind were piled high the first time I walked in—especially those of elk and mule deer, but also whitetail deer, moose, and European fallow deer—with some having already been selected and partially assembled into chandeliers and other items.

This successful business is owned by entrepreneur Brant Davis, who is an unlikely and unashamed combination of antler lover and former ski bum. Over the duration of a year or so I often stopped by to talk with Brant and his fellow artisans Mat Snyder and Paul Luczah. It was here that I began to realize just how dynamic the antler-fabrication market had become in recent years. Chandeliers and other antler-furniture items from this shop have recently found their way into the homes of an NFL quarterback, a leading American fashion designer, and presidents of NBC and Pepsi, as well as estates located in Jackson Hole, Aspen, San Francisco, Lake Placid, and elsewhere—including, of course, many Ellicottville chalets.

Gone Wild's business headquarters and a second gallery are now located in a storefront on the main street through town. Brant's intention when laying out the gallery was to create a warm atmosphere where passersby and potential customers could just hang out on Friday

No two antlers are alike, and assembling antlers for fabricating into an item can require an artistic sense of shape and form. Here Brant Davis considers the symmetries presented by five moose antlers while constructing a chandelier at his company, "Gone Wild Creations" in Ellicottville, New York (www.gonewildcreations.com).

and Saturday evenings. (Remember, this is a ski town!) Here, visitors and local friends can enjoy free beer, listen to music, and talk with the craftsmen about antlers while trying to visualize how such-and-such a style of chandelier or lamp stand might fit best into their décor. To me, it seems like the ideal environment for antler lovers.

There are several other antler-furniture and antler-fixture companies around the country, operating mostly on the Internet and in ski towns. Regardless of where they come from, however, professionally made antler products can be very expensive. For example, a custom-made, electrified, 24-light chandelier constructed from a combination of elk and moose antlers standing 72 inches high and 72 inches wide might sell for $40,000. At the lower end of a typical price range, an 18 x 30-inch, three-light chandelier priced over a thousand dollars will sell quickly. There are honest reasons for these high prices, beginning with the already high costs of large antlers. But just being large isn't enough; every antler must match in size and symmetry those others that you

Top view of a spiral of moose antlers for the bottom layer of a chandelier.
These antlers have been colored with wood stain for uniformity of appearance.

might plan to use in the same fabrication. Then there's the problem (as explained below) that most chandelier designs require the antlers along the outer rims to be either all left-sided or all right-sided. It's for reasons such as these that a professional antler fabricator must have deep piles of expensive antlers on hand at all times. Finally, art carries a price; the assembly of antlers into a dramatically beautiful chandelier is the art of the sculptor.

So, for the amateur antler craftsman, it can be a long, scary leap to try to reach the level of quality on a single item that a professional is able to routinely produce in quantity. But that's no reason not to try. On the following pages I describe the fundamental details of how to make a chandelier, and I also provide many "can-do" suggestions for smaller antlercraft projects.

AMATEUR ANTLERCRAFT

Making neat stuff from deer antlers is not a new idea! Ever since one of our first ancestors picked up a shed antler to scratch his back (or *her* back!), antlers have been used in one way or another by humankind as tools and decorations. Today, people are still using antlers to make chandeliers, functional furniture such as coffee tables, knives, door handles, buttons, and jewelry. Just a decade or two ago, the use of anything made from animal parts was well on the way to becoming politically incorrect, even if you were only going to eat or wear it. Antlers are now back in style for rustic decorations in theme restaurants and ski lodges, but even this is nothing new: antler chandeliers hung in the baronial estates of Europe several centuries ago . . . although the light switches on the walls never worked right.

The popularity of antlers and antlercraft has grown right along with the national interest in using materials from renewable, natural sources. I see this in part as being a backlash against our throwaway,

Antlers are a renewable resource that come in all sizes and shapes, which means a fabricator must stockpile large numbers of them to find just the right ones to fit a planned design.

instant-gratification society. Computer-controlled machines can in seconds produce high-quality items that might take us hours or even weeks to make by hand. Sometimes we may wonder, What is the point? We want very much to be involved in the creative process; we get pleasure out of using our hands. If we contemplate and then commit to actually creating something useful and beautiful from natural materials such as antlers, we can force the passage of time to slow down to a trickle of comprehensible minutes and then, finally, we can begin to even feel ourselves breathing.

Antlers don't come as the parts of a kit. There's no such kit on the market because, like fingerprints, every antler is different. Consequently, you won't find antlers in any sort of pre-measured form. There are no dotted lines that say "cut here" and no exploded drawings that show you how to insert end A into socket B. There isn't even a customer service telephone number or a website where you can ask for advice. Nope, when it comes to antlercraft, you're on your own. Putting a project together requires a good eye and an artful hand—and sometimes three or four hands at once.

FORM, FUNCTION, AND THE GOLDEN MEAN
You can use ordinary woodworking tools for doing antlercraft. Antlers are even stronger than wood, and they are easily as machineable as hardwood oak. Most work very nicely in chandeliers, as furniture legs and struts, and in various tools, handles, and decorations. While these particular applications might seem a bit inappropriate—perhaps even disrespectful—uses of antlers, keep in mind that the natural beauty of antlers is not decreased by their being incorporated into the design of something else. Also, most antlers that are used in this sort of fabrication have been found as annual sheds and the deer or elk that dropped them is probably still alive.

The natural "design" of individual antlers (especially whitetail antlers) often seems to adhere to the pleasing proportions of the "Golden Ratio," which is seen throughout nature and has been applied often in human art. For some reason not yet explained fully by science, the proportion of 0.62 to 1 is in some ways more pleasing to the human eye than 1 to 1. For example, on the ancient statue of the Venus de Milo, the navel is located at a point 62 percent of the way up, not at 50 percent as with the rest of us ordinary humans. I have a small whitetail antler on my desk next to the keyboard where I'm writing this book. It helps me focus on the subject, and I can use it to stab at anyone who interrupts me. The first tine is 4 1/2 inches long, and it sprouts from the main beam about 7 1/2 inches from the tip of the antler. That's an approximate ratio of 0.6, and the antler looks "just right" to me. I'm reasonably certain that you would agree. The remaining tines are shorter as the tip of the antler is approached, and the same ratio of tine length to distance is maintained for each one. (You can see this illustrated on page 194 in the idealized side-view sketch of a typical whitetail antler on the Boone and Crockett score sheet.)

Countless other examples of the Golden Ratio (also called the Golden Mean) are found in such diverse things as the location of spots on a moth's wing, the designs of some modern automobiles, the patterns of leaves on a vine, and even the placements and widths of human teeth in a friendly smile. The same proportion that defines the Golden Mean can also be used to plot a spiral . . . but not just an ordinary one. The curve of a Nautilus seashell best demonstrates the expanding spiral of the Golden Mean, but it also appears in almost every ordered natural growth, from the locations of seeds in sunflower blossoms to the sweep of bighorn sheep horns and the arc of antelope horns. And if I hold this deer antler, the one on my desk, in just the right position in which an opposing buck might view it, I can see the main beam as a beginning spiral.

My point here is that well-formed antlers are naturally beautiful to the human eye; the art is already there, even before we attempt to combine it with other shapes and planes. A good antler chandelier can bring out the best features of the antlers from which it was made. We are capable of perceiving this beauty, but we don't entirely understand why it appeals so strongly to us. Apparently it's all in the math.

On a smaller scale of antlercraft, such as in the making of knife handles, our sense of touch comes into play. A knife should be "ergonomically correct" by providing us with a good grip and a downward curvature that places the blade in position for easier cutting without straining your wrist. The main beams of whitetail and mule deer and the tines of elk antlers seem almost designed by nature to serve as handles for knives and other utensils. There are no strict rules for where to cut that special section of antler to use for a solid handle, but your hand will know it when it feels it. The Golden Ratio works also for the design and manufacture of knives. That is, if the ratio of blade length (or handle length) to the total length of the knife is 0.62 to 1, the odds are good that you'll feel that the finished knife has a beautifully balanced appearance.

FABRICATING AN ANTLER CHANDELIER

Building an antler chandelier is not something you can do in just a couple of hours. You *really* slow time down when you put one together! At a glance, it might look like an easy project, but it turns out to be difficult from the first step: getting all the antlers into position so that they both look good and are well-balanced. The good news is that you can use ordinary household tools for most of the work.

Tools

You need the following items:
- handsaw
- electric drill with drill bits
- a few hex-head lag screws
- a large eye-lag screw
- socket wrench
- masking tape
- epoxy
- decorator chain (from which to hang the finished chandelier)
- wires and sockets of whatever wiring system that you'll install
- high-speed rotary tool as described in Chapter 7 (optional)

An artistic sense of what looks good can be a real help here, too, because a poorly assembled antler chandelier can resemble a bad roadkill. I haven't specified the various sizes of drill bits and other hardware because those will vary depending on what kind of antler will be used and the size and number of antlers.

Antlers

At minimum, you'll need at least six antlers, all close to the same size, and all from the same side of the heads of six deer. Right here is where most well-intentioned plans to make a chandelier hit the dirt. After all, just obtaining six left-side deer antlers (for example) all about the same size and configuration, can be far more difficult than the fabrication itself. If you're an experienced shed-hunter and your idea of the ultimate accomplishment is to find six years' worth of shed antlers all from the same side of the same buck's head . . . well, in six short years you could drive yourself totally crazy. On the other hand, you can avoid that (and maybe even save your marriage, too) by buying the needed antlers on eBay or from other online sources. Whitetail antlers tend to dominate those markets, with mule deer coming in a strong second and elk not far behind. Moose antlers are a lesser possibility, but they make

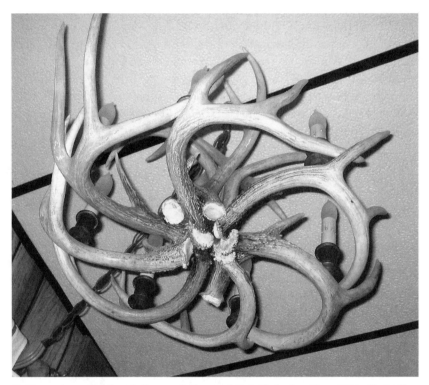

Bottom view of a chandelier made from whitetail shed antlers. Note that all seven antlers are "right-handed" in order to form the full circle without interruption. This chandelier was created by Len Nagel, proprietor of the Antler Shed.

a splendid foundation on which to build with deer antlers. If the chandelier you have in mind is intended for a room that you'll be living in, be sure to consider whether there will be room for you *and* the chandelier at the same time. A trophy elk antler can be as big as a bicycle and weigh almost as much, and if you don't think that a chandelier as big as six bicycles tied together will quite go with the décor, you might consider downsizing.

Design

Antler chandeliers come in a thousand different designs, but the majority of them fall into one of the following four main styles:

Upside-down umbrella. This is the most common style for whitetail and mule deer antlers. The butt-ends of several antlers are joined together in the middle, and the tines point upward around the edge of the bowl that's formed. There is only one level (or "tier") in this design, but if the antlers are well-matched in size, the appearance can be particularly striking. With tightly curved antlers, the chandelier will almost take the shape of a globe. A handsome flared version of this chandelier can be created from larger antlers that are allowed to sag somewhat from the center attachment.

Cascade. A cascaded chandelier starts out the same as the umbrella described above, but second and even third tiers of smaller antlers are added in rings, the end result somewhat resembling a Christmas tree. At all levels the antler tines point upward. This design works best with whitetail and mule deer antlers because the nice, tight curves of the main beams are well-displayed. Still, most cascades for sale are built with small elk antlers. Symmetry is important here; otherwise, the chandelier resembles a pile of tossed antlers.

Fleur-de-leis. This is the French national symbol. If you can't visualize it right at this moment, just think of a half-peeled banana held upright. We are talking about a chandelier that could be 3 to 5 feet tall and worth between $2,000 and $7,000. (If I err in price here, it would be on the low side.) On the bottom tier of this design, the tines are aimed slightly downward around the outside edge. In the center, a narrow column of antlers sprouts upward toward the ceiling. This design is best done with the relatively long elk antlers, at least in the center column, but it also easily incorporates the antlers of other species as well. Moose antlers, being as large as they are, can ably form the bottom layer with only three antlers.

Wagon wheel. The basic wagon wheel design is an old standby, and it has probably been around since wagon wheels were invented. An actual wagon wheel is hung from the ceiling and kept securely in a horizontal position by three cables fastened at 120 degrees around the rim of the wheel. Antlers are then fastened in whatever positions please your eye. A significant improvement in this circular design that doesn't include a wagon wheel has recently become particularly popular: a large circle that would have been the rim of the wheel is instead constructed from individual antlers, which are laid more or less horizontally in an overlapping pattern and then securely bolted into place. The trick here is to hide the connections while ensuring a rigid construction. Fallow deer antlers work very well for constructing the basic circle. Elk antlers can then be used to tie the whole chandelier together and to provide a connection for hanging from the ceiling. Generally, the butt-ends of the elk antlers meet high in the center of the circle.

A modification of the wagon wheel design involves uses a vertical wood post as a wagon axle from which the antlers sprout as wheel "spokes." This piece was made by Eric Carr; you can see more examples at www.crookedcreekantlerart.com.

Assembling a Chandelier

Let's start with the least complex chandelier, the upside-down umbrella. We'll use whitetail antlers. Remember, the six antlers you use must be all left-sided or all right-sided.

1. Begin by placing the antlers in a closely grouped circle, with the butt ends down on your work surface and in contact with each other. (Eventually, you will be lag-bolting the butt-ends together.) With the thicker regions of the main beams in contact with the work surface, the tines will be pointed toward the ceiling. Ideally, the natural curve of the main beams will combine to form an outside circle. Use the masking tape to hold each antler in contact with its neighbors on either side. The idea here is to play with the different combinations of antlers to develop a pleasing symmetry. This might take longer than you would think. In fact, you might decide at this point that your antlers aren't quite as matched as you thought they were, or that you need yet another

*Bottom view of a whitetail antler chandelier in which the antlers in the
bottom layer are spread separately instead of maintaining contact. Not fully
visible here are two more antlers that sprout vertically from the center of the
assembly.*

antler or two, or that you have too many. You might even decide
that you'd be better off just buying an antler chandelier outright.
(Ha! If the antlers you're working with are anywhere close to
being respectably sized, you'll spend approximately a thousand
dollars or more to buy what you can make yourself. Shall we get
back to work now?)

Sometimes it's necessary to saw one or two of the antler butt-
ends an inch or so short in order to get both a good fit down
there and an attractive appearance higher up. Once you've
adjusted the antlers for the thousandth time and like the final
result, tightly bind them all into place with more of the masking tape.

2. Fasten the butt-ends of the antlers together with several $1/4$ x 3-
inch-long hex-head lag screws. To do this, you'll need to first

The butt-ends of antlers are connected to each other at the center of the chandelier. This is done by drilling and counter-boring so that the fastened nuts and bolts are completely below the antler surface. Mix the shavings from drilling with epoxy and use the resulting paste to cover and hide the hardware.

drill the holes and then counter-bore $3/4$-inch diameter recesses so that the hex-heads can be turned with a socket wrench to a depth flush with the surfaces of the antlers. Save all the drill shavings. When you're finally satisfied that the antlers are tightly lagged and secure enough, mix up a thick paste of epoxy and the antler shavings, and use that to fill the counter-bored recesses.

3. Install the hanger near the middle of the connected butts. For a whitetail chandelier, a $3/8$ x 8-inch lag screw with either a closed eye or an open hook will be sufficient. This requires that another hole to be drilled (vertically this time) so that the hanger can be screwed into place. Tilting can be a real problem if the weight distribution of the antlers isn't well-centered. One remedy for this is to bend the long-shanked lag screw in whatever direction is necessary to achieve a balanced chandelier. This "easy" step might require a couple hours of your time, not including the time spent driving back to the hardware store for more gear.

4. Wiring the antler chandelier for lighting can be done in several different ways. The most difficult method involves drilling $1/4$-inch tunnels all the way from the center of the chandelier, where the hanger is affixed, to where you want the lights to be positioned. One type of drill bit that's particularly suitable for this task is a $1/4$ x 18-inch-long "bell-hanger installer" that has a special hole in the flute to which the slender wire can be attached

This elk-antler "cascade" chandelier is now ready for installation of the long-shanked lag screw for hanging. The long shank serves dual purposes: it can be more easily bent to the true center of gravity, and it helps prevent tilting.

for pulling backward through the new hole. If you come to a bend in the road that requires that the drill bit emerges and a second tunnel be drilled along the rest of the curve, then so be it. Again, keep the shavings for more epoxy-pasting.

Another, slightly easier method is to use a rotary tool to rout a groove along the top surface of each antler where a light is wanted. This can be covered and hidden with commercial wood putty and then stained. The least desirable way would be to tack the wire along the top of each antler as needed. If this chandelier is a project that's never going to leave home, then fine—do it the easy way. But remember, if you're harboring secret thoughts about selling your chandelier on the online market, by all means do the best job you can of drilling hidden tunnels!

5. Installation of the actual lighting fixtures requires that you drill vertically at each location to be lighted and then counter-bore from the top in such a way as is required for whichever type of lighting you're using. There are as many ways to do this as there

The balance of the finished chandelier is checked by artisan Paul Luczah of Gone Wild Creations. Most antler chandeliers have a "good side" from which they appear most symmetrical, and it's from that perspective that balancing should be done.

are light bulb types on the market. Traditional Christmas tree bulbs are often used for antler chandeliers, but if the lighting is intended to illuminate a room in addition to decorating it, bulbs with higher wattages are needed. Imitation candles and even little lamp-shaded lights are popular. Little globe-shaped light bulbs can help offset problems with tilt, because they always appear to be upright.

So . . . what might your finished antler chandelier be worth on the online market? Whoa, you say, it's not for sale! OK, OK, calm down. But what about the second one that you might make next week? The dogs are whining for food and your babies need diapers . . . well, maybe not *your* babies, but just remember that there's a hot market for handcrafted antler items.

"CAN-DO" ITEMS

This book is not intended to show all the "How-to-Do-It" details of antlercraft. Instead, it's a "Can-Do" book that's intended to acquaint you with what other people are doing with antlers, in the hopes that each of us will learn something we didn't already know. The following list gives a number of antlercraft possibilities.

Belt Buckle	Christmas Tree	Drawer Handles
Bird Feeder	Coat Rack	Dream Catcher
Candelabra	Coffee Table Legs	Fireplace Tool Holder
Cane Handle	Cribbage Board	Gearshift Knob
Chair	Door Handles	Genealogical Tree

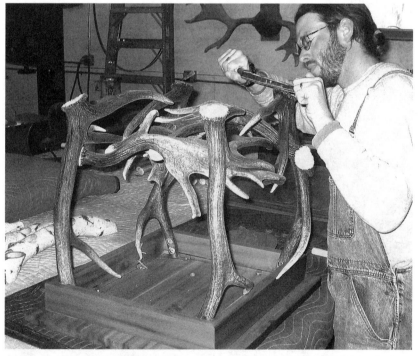

Antler furniture décor obviously matches well with antler chandeliers. Artisan Mat Snyder of Gone Wild Creations files off a rough spot for even-footing of a coffee table. Antlers are naturally shaped for load bearing in the wild and are well-suited for this kind of support application.

Globe Holder
Guitar Bridge
Gun Rack
Hat Rack
Knife Handle
Lamp Stand
Lampshade Finial
Picture Frame
Pistol Grips
Plate Display
Razor Handle
Shotgun Butt Plate
Silverware Handles
Toilet Paper Holder
Towel Rack
Wall Sconce Lamp
Wreath

Hand-tooled hunting knife with combination of Brazilian rosewood and whitetail antler-coronet handle, made by Frank A. Johnston of Silverdale, Washington, and currently owned by Jerry Paduano of Ashville, New York.

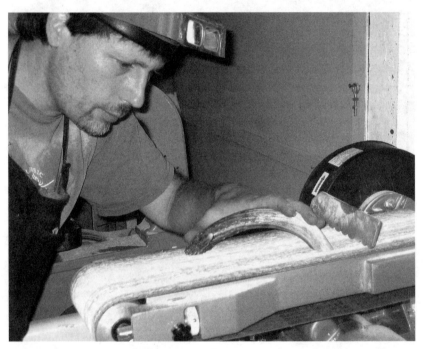

Jack Brown, known as the "Bonecarver" on eBay, uses a belt sander to form an antler door handle.

*Jody Finch Cowan, marketing director of the
National Whitetail Deer Education Foundation
and events organizer for Deerassic Park, models a
"bear tooth" necklace made from the tips of whitetail antler tines.*

9

ANTLER ART: FROM CAVE WALLS TO THE INTERNET

We value antlers in many ways. To collectors, the value of antlers can be directly measured in money as well as in the simpler pleasures of owning and displaying such naturally beautiful objects. Trophy hunters and shed-hunters are able to find value in their personal involvement with and acquisition of antlers, which carries over into the hobbyist fields of antler carving and fabrication as well. Even thousands of years ago, humans valued antlers as tools, decorations—and the subjects of art on cave walls.

The following pages contain eight beautiful examples of sculpture, drawing, carving, and painting that in each case is directly focused on antlers. Antler-related art objects have always been popular, but over just the last twenty years or so, as antlers (particularly sheds) have become more available to non-hunters, there has been a significant growth of antler art. The antlers of fully adult deer are generally much larger than is necessary for physical performance; they're mostly for show, a demonstration of the ability to be larger than needed—almost a form of "conspicuous consumption." They are dramatic in appearance, they are symbolic of competition and strength, and in possessing them in any form we feel a genuine connection to the wild world. Considering all this, how could there *not* be a category of art devoted just to antlers?

Good Genes (detail)

COLE JOHNSON (www.colejohnsonart.com)
Graphite powder sketch

By incorporating powdered graphite into his pencil sketches, Cole Johnson creates a certain mood and captures the softness of hair and faint shadows. The use of an eraser in the later stages of the drawing adds light and gives shape to the subject. Although the black, gray, and white of graphite art might at first appear to some people as simply colorless, there is depth and subtlety to be found in Johnson's sketches that can make colored drawings seem too sweetly sugared.

Humming Bird

LARRY BAESLER (www.elkfoundation.org)
Miniature sculpture from elk antler and bone

Artist Larry Baesler is the lands program director of the Rocky Mountain Elk Foundation. In another life, he obviously could have been a successful full-time artist, but his wildlife scenes—composed of pieces of antler and bone that all seem to tell a story—are actually the products of a part-time hobbyist. Baesler selects pieces of antler on the basis of shape, color, and texture, always attempting to take advantage of those characteristics that are most like the object or animal to be formed. For example, eyes can be made from dark antelope horn. In the picture shown here, the body of the hummingbird was first formed from a single piece of antler using a rotary tool. The wings were taken from a portion of an antler with a texture and color different from the hummingbird's body. Super glue mixed with antler dust was used to bind and blend the various parts together. Most of Baesler's scenes are miniatures of 1:5 scale and are approximately 6 x 6 x 6 inches.

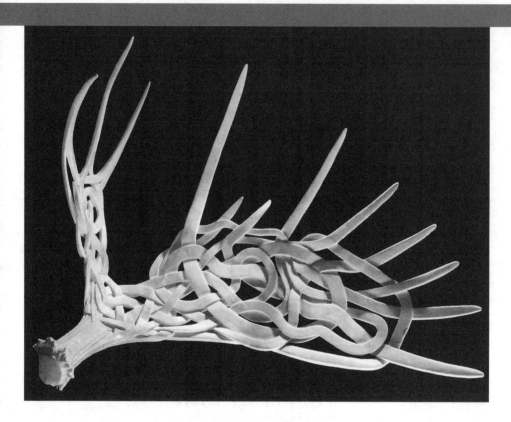

Celtic Confusion

SHANE WILSON (www.shanewilson.com)
Moose antler sculpture

S hane Wilson is a sculptor who lives and works in the remote central region of Canada's Yukon Territory. He specializes in the carving of antler, tusk, and ancient ivory. He also teaches a summer course in antler carving with rotary tools at Red Deer University and other venues. His website includes several step-by-step photographs of the process of sculpting *Celtic Confusion*, which would be very helpful to beginning carvers.

Wapiti Approaching with Lowered Antlers

ANTHONY BUBENIK (deceased)
Graphite sketch for a scientific report

The late Dr. Tony Bubenik was a wildlife biologist specializing in the physiology and social behavior of deer species for the Ontario Wildlife Research Institute. Bubenik was both a world-renowned authority and a natural artist who could translate the physical details of deer physiology into the poetry of motion, as was done in this sketch of a wild elk. As remarkable as this sketch is, it was not intended to be art for art's sake, but instead as a more accurate rendition of how a bull elk holds its antlers low on his body when approaching a female elk. Photography is not always the best way to illustrate that kind of subtle behavior.

Totem

AYAL HAUSFELD (ayalhausfeld@yahoo.com)
Burlap and jeweler's wax on driftwood

To some eyes, this miniature statue of an antlered human symbolizes the anguish of bearing the burdens of competitiveness and authority that antlers represent. To the young artist himself, *Totem* describes a personal and archetypal transition from childhood into adulthood, and from isolation into communion. Hausfeld is an art therapist who lives in Boulder, and he often explores the Colorado mountainsides in search of shed antlers. (In Hebrew, "Ayal" means deer.)

Antlered Whitetail on Driftwood

EARL C. MARTZ (814-927-8659)
Combination of sculpting, casting, and painting

Particularly when seen in real life, this work of art is an eye-catcher. An interesting piece of driftwood transitions gradually and naturally, almost impressionistically, into the antlered head of a whitetail deer. The sculpted and cast deer appears very much alive and natural in that setting, just as real deer in the wild are seemingly able to materialize out of thin air, once you know what to look for. This miniature sculpture is approximately 1:3 scale. The artist, Earl Martz, has developed his artistic ability from a background of printing, carving, and taxidermy. He lives in the Cook Forest of northwestern Pennsylvania.

The Trackers

JACK PALUH (www.jackpaluh.com)
Oil painting

The title of this painting is difficult to understand when you first look at it. There's an antlered buck hiding in the shelter of snow-covered pines. Sure, you can see the tracks of hoof marks on the log beside the buck, but . . . suddenly, unexpectedly, you spot the first tracker only a dozen yards behind the deer, so close that it startles you. Then you see a second man further back; it is this second hunter who will probably have a better chance at a killing shot when the buck leaps out of hiding and races to get downwind of the trackers. The artist, Jack Paluh, is himself an experienced Pennsylvania deer hunter, and he understands both the drama and the techniques of tracking a deer in snow.

Squash Spirit, 1984

**STANLEY HILL (deceased; for details on other artwork,
contact his son Russell at 716-773-4974.)
Moose-antler sculpture**

This moose-antler carving is in the collection of the Iroquois Indian Museum in Howe's Cave, New York, by arrangement with the Hill family. Stanley Hill was a Mohawk Indian of the Iroquois Confederacy. He spent most of his working life as an iron worker and later as the co-owner of a construction company. The loss of one of his sons impelled him to look for meaning in ways that transcended the corporate existence, and he discovered that he was a natural bone-and-antler carver. *Squash Spirit, 1984* has a serenity that keeps me turning back to the book in which it appears, *The Spirit Released: A Circle Complete*. Hill's works are now on display in several museums and galleries in the northeastern United States.

10

THE FUTURE OF ANTLERS

Will we all still be as bonkers about antlers in the future as we are now? Yes, I think so, and maybe we'll be even *more* interested in them, and a lot of new people will have joined us. As we've seen, Cabela's and Bass Pro Shops have invested millions of dollars over just the last few years to buy Boone and Crockett Club–certified whitetail and mule deer antlers, and that's a pretty good indication of where this whole thing is headed—they'll never let us forget antlers even if we wanted to. Antler-lovers apparently have much to look forward to in the coming years: there are several ongoing events and programs that will continue to feed the fires of our enthusiasm, all of which are described in this chapter. Fact is, the antler craze is really just beginning and as more people realize what you and I already know about antlers, they'll get crazy too.

Whether we are big-game hunters, shed-hunters, carvers, artisans, natural history buffs, collectors, or dealers (or one of the many possible overlapped combinations), one thing we have in common is a desire to continue having antlers be available to us. Things look good for us . . . but what really is the future of antlers in North America? As the enthusiasm and interest continue to develop over the next decade, will there continue to be a healthy supply of new antlers to feed our needs? Read on.

COLD, HARD ANTLERS

Just as we would deal with cold, hard cash, let's talk practically about the factors influencing antler availability and price levels in the coming years. If we were putting our spare money into the stock market and were heavily invested in the manufacture of wool clothing, for example, we would be keenly interested in anything that might affect the well-being of sheep. As antler collectors, carvers, fabricators, artists, and hunters, the ways in which the populations of deer, elk, caribou, and moose are managed by state wildlife departments are very much our business. Beginning late in the last century and continuing through this one, the antler boom has been supported in part by a relative abundance of antlers, especially those of deer and elk. Since the 1970s, the whitetail population in America has been doubling roughly every decade. There is already an informal antler market where prices per pound fluctuate according to supply and demand, and these prices are routinely reported in fur-trapper publications. The shifts in the availability of one species' antlers affects the prices of all the other species. Within the recent past, a long, hard winter in the western states reduced the elk population, and those bulls that survived had generally smaller antlers the next summer—a typical response of a male deer to winter stress and a poor diet in early spring. Consequently, the price of shed elk antlers went sky-high; the carvers and other artisans began looking for lower-priced whitetail and mule deer antlers, and then these rose in price, too.

There are other factors besides herd population that are influencing the prices of antlers. The American elk herd, for example, is being managed to fit the decreasing acreage of wilderness area that is available to the elk and protected from housing development. The Rocky Mountain Elk Foundation estimates that the current range of elk habitat is a mere 10 percent of what it was two hundred years ago. The elk population has also increased relative to its shrinking habitat, and there's been more elk-to-human eye contact than ever before. Whereas whitetail deer (and moose, too) seemingly could live in a Wal-Mart parking lot feeding off gum wrappers and cigarette butts, the typical elk can't tolerate the presence of humans and will run to the next county when it hears your car door slam. Consequently, wildlife managers have been forced to increase the number of tags available to elk hunters. Antler size and availability have both declined. My research on the Boone and Crockett online database reveals a downward trend in median elk antler size over the past fifty years. There's no reason to believe that the trend will reverse itself.

Looking at the grouped five-year averages, we see there has been a drop of over 10 inches from the early 1950s (386 inches average) to the turn of the century (less than 376 inches). There was a slight blip upward in the 1970s, but the overall trend for the median values is toward smaller antlers. By the way, if 10 inches doesn't sound like much to you, consider this: if the ten tines on a "five-by-five" bull were each cut an inch shorter, you'd be looking at an obviously smaller rack.

The reason that elk antlers are smaller today is probably that the average age of the bulls is less than it used to be and is still trending

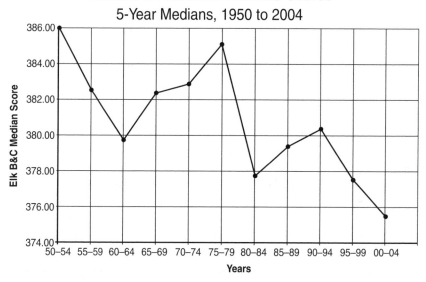

Decline of American Elk B&C Scores
5-Year Medians, 1950 to 2004

downward. This is due to the culling of the larger (older) trophy bucks that results from increased pressure from licensed hunters. An elk doesn't grow its biggest antlers until around eight to ten years of age. (Whitetails develop their best antlers at half that age.) Don't get me wrong here: this isn't currently something the antler carver or artisan should get alarmed about. Trophy hunters and collectors have more cause for immediate concern. Still, the situation deserves the continuing attention of all of us.

THE WHITETAIL DOE-TO-BUCK RATIO

Male/female ratios are highly variable from region to region, sometimes even from township to township. The pre-hunt ratio of adult does to bucks is used by professional wildlife managers as an indicator of the balance and productivity of a whitetail deer herd. By productivity, I mean the ability of the general deer population to replenish itself via the birth and survival of fawns. In terms of reproductive efficiency, a healthy herd will on average be a youthful herd with just average antlers. Scientists have modeled the theoretical life histories of deer and are reasonably sure that the North American whitetail doe-to-buck ratio before Columbus arrived was about 1.3:1—one and one-third does for every buck, or four does for every three bucks.

Let's now consider a more lopsided ratio of 2:1. This would mean that there are two adult does for every one adult buck or, stated another way, that the herd is 66.7 percent does and 33.3 percent bucks. (The fawns, which aren't included in this ratio, will be very close to equal in numbers of male and females.) From a reproductive standpoint, even 2:1 could be considered to be a reasonably healthy ratio, because a buck can and does breed more than one doe during the course of the rut. Even a 1:1 ratio wouldn't mean that the bucks and does would pair off as though at a Saturday night square dance; instead, the dominant buck would take most of the girls home.

While the whitetail deer population has grown enormously over the last several decades, the male percentage of it has dwindled in some areas down to a distinct minority from the extended effect of hunting seasons that are mainly bucks-only. An imbalance now exists in many areas of the U.S., and during the rut, there may be ten does in heat to be bred by the one dominant buck in a brief period of time. So, while we might view this as a fantasy situation for the male deer, the fact is that many female deer simply don't breed. But the real bummer in this situation, as far as antler development is concerned, is that many of the lesser bucks get the opportunity to pass along their inferior genes—even a little fork-horn buck that might be a carrier of small-antler genes no matter how old or otherwise physically healthy he might be. What's lacking in this scenario is the competition between fully adult bucks that naturally selects for physical strength and larger antlers. What's needed to improve the genetic worth of the overall herd is open competition among mature bucks that have been allowed to survive long enough to be in the big leagues, where push-and-shove is the name of the game.

According to Keith McCaffery, a Wisconsin deer biologist who lectures nationally on deer population factors and who was one of the main consultants for this chapter, it's generally assumed that bucks are killed in roughly the same percentages across the adult deer age classes. Consequently, the percentage of yearlings killed reflects the annual overall mortality rate for all bucks. This isn't rocket science, but it gets complicated. According to surveys of bucks killed in Wisconsin, the age distribution for adult bucks when hunters first step into the woods on Opening Day is:

70%	Yearlings ($1\frac{1}{2}$ to $2\frac{1}{2}$ years old; usually spike bucks or fork-horns)
20%	Mature Bucks ($2\frac{1}{2}$ to $3\frac{1}{2}$ years old; usually 6 or 8 slender tines)
10%	Prime Bucks ($3\frac{1}{2}$ years and older; usually considered to have trophy status)

As a hunter, these percentagess are the approximate odds that you face for dropping a wall-hanger buck. That is, it would be if all those tracks in the snow were made by bucks . . . but they're not. This is why the autumn ratio of does to bucks is worth understanding whether you're a big-game hunter or a shed-hunter.

Imagine a ratio of 1.5:1, which would be the same as 60 does and 40 bucks per 100 deer. Here's an example of what the breakdown is for the numbers and ages of the pre-hunt bucks:

60 DOES	40 BUCKS
	70% × 40 = 28 Yearlings
	20% × 40 = 8 Mature Bucks per 100 deer
	10% × 40 = 4 Prime Bucks per 100 deer

At the 1.5:1 ratio, out of a total of 100 deer, only four bucks would be worthy of trophy status, and only another eight would have respectable antlers. If the deer density where you'll be hunting next fall were 25 deer per square mile with a well-balanced 1.5:1, then there would be only one trophy buck and two respectable bucks per square mile.

By the end of the hunting season, approximately only a third of the bucks will still be alive. Obviously, the dead bucks don't shed, but their antlers will still enter the supply chain for mounting, collecting, and antlercraft. The bucks still living are the ones that will be shedding the antlers that the shed-hunters eagerly seek. Using that same population that we started out with, here's what the numbers would look like per square mile, before and after the hunting season:

NUMBER OF BUCKS PER SQUARE MILE

AGE	PRE-SEASON	POST-SEASON
Yearling	7	2.3
Mature	2	0.7
Prime	1	0.3

Please note that the proportions that I've shown here probably won't hold tightly once so-called "quality deer management" antler restrictions are applied. (See page 181.) Studies are now showing that "antler point restrictions" (APRs) that disallow the harvesting of smaller-antlered whitetail deer may actually result in an increase in $2\frac{1}{2}$-year-old bucks, along with a corresponding decrease in trophy bucks $3\frac{1}{2}$ years and older because of the increased pressure on them.

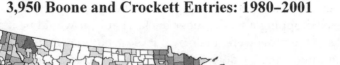

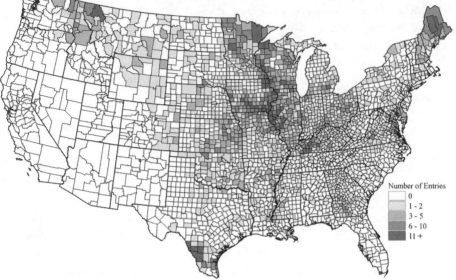

This map was created by Joel Helmer for the Boone and Crockett Club. It shows the concentrations by county of 3,950 B&C-registered whitetail bucks from 1980 to 2001. There are several factors that can help explain why the upper Mississippi Basin, southern Texas, and certain other areas produce so many trophy bucks, but one thing they all have in common is soil that is rich in lime, nitrogen, phosphorus, and potassium.

THE INCREDIBLE SHRINKING WHITETAIL ANTLERS

The declining population of older trophy bucks isn't the only problem facing antler collectors. As with elk, trophy whitetail antlers have been steadily getting smaller since around 1970. This applies to both typical and non-typical antlers, and on top of that, for some reason that so far defies full explanation, the percentage of whitetail deer that have non-typical antlers also has gradually decreased.

The changes in score wouldn't be statistically significant from just one year to the next, but over the past thirty years, median scores have steadily dropped an average of about $\frac{1}{8}$ inch per year, from around $174\frac{1}{2}$ down to $170\frac{1}{2}$ inches—a huge change. Four inches might not seem like much, but we're talking thousands of deer here. Something is occurring in the Boone and Crockett Club trophy whitetail population that is causing the median, that "halfway point," to shift downward.

This shift might not be a problem, perhaps just an interesting puzzle, but it could also indicate a worsening of deer habitat and nutrition. There are more deer concentrated in smaller areas today than the period from the 1950s through to the 1980s. Higher concentrations of deer (usually 20 or 30 per square mile in decent deer habitat, but in some extreme cases 50 or more per square mile) places pressure on the carrying capacity of the habitat and food supply even under the most favorable conditions. We all know that a healthy buck with proper nutrition will grow larger antlers than one that is not getting the proper amount of nutrients. The forests of the East had been logged off until the 1940s and in some cases the 1950s, and during the early 1950s they were recovering from this heavy onslaught. For the next twenty to thirty years, there was a large amount of brush that provided better food and escape cover than today's forests, which consist mostly of mature growth. The acreage being farmed has dropped dramatically since the 1950s, and croplands provide deer with high-nutrient foods that don't naturally occur in abundance in the wild. Also, prior to the 1950s, many states had no deer seasons.

Still, the most obvious probable cause of declining scores is what I proposed for elk: the average age of the trophy-class bucks is declining, and with it, the potential for large antler growth. Frankly, most whitetail deer hunters these days have probably never even *seen* a deer in the wild sporting the huge antlers that virtually any well-fed 3 ½-year-old buck is easily capable of growing. Those who have seen one are still talking about it. The problem is, due to hunting pressure, only about 4 percent of bucks ever get that old, according to researchers in Pennsylvania. Considering that whitetail deer can normally live 8 to 10 years or more, the relatively short lives of today's bucks create a sorry situation from the perspective of antler development. It's now known that whitetail bucks can reach optimum antler development as early as age 4 ½ with the right combination of diet, low population density, and really good genes. Generally, whitetail bucks that qualify for Boone and Crockett Club status are 5 ½ years or older, but ironically, the current World Record holder (the 1993 Milo Hanson buck) was only 4 ½. As bucks get older than 6 ½ or 7 ½, the tines and main beams become shorter and blunter, and the lower regions of the main beam gain thickness. Of course, most of us wouldn't know that from personal observation!

A recent archeological study of over three thousand deer jaw bones dug from the middens (communal trash dumps) of Native Americans has revealed the age structure of whitetail herds in the time before European settlement. Back then, when deer were harvested for meat

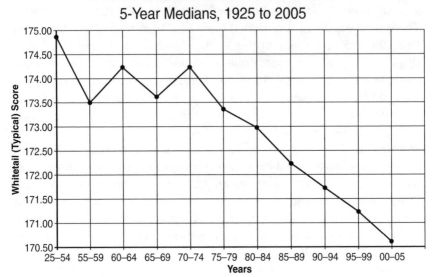

Decline of Whitetail Deer B&C Scores
5-Year Medians, 1925 to 2005

instead of antlers, there were seven times as many deer 4 ½ and older as there would be today in the same herd. Let's put that another way; the jawbone study showed that over 30 percent of pre-European bucks were 4 ½ older, compared to less than 5 percent today. Recreating that same age-profile in today's deer herds is achievable, but it would require that the buck hunting seasons essentially be closed for a number of years. It's a hot issue. It's a complex subject. And get this: it's all about antlers, those strange-looking bones that grow out of a deer's head. Are we crazy or what?

Even while median trophy scores have gone down, the number of trophy bucks has risen. The whitetail deer population in the United States and Canada has been growing steadily for several decades. So has the sheer number of bucks that would score more than the entry-level score of 160 inches needed to be registered by Boone and Crockett Club. The table on the next page lists the number of typical whitetail bucks registered for each five-year group since 1960 and includes a breakdown of just those bucks that scored from the entry level of 160 inches up to just under 170 inches. Note that the percentage of bucks in this category has increased greatly over the past decades. The last column lists the average of the top five individual World Record scores within each five-year period, and it shows that there are no apparent trends over time at the top end of the trophy range.

INCREASE SINCE 1960 IN BOONE AND CROCKETT
ENTRY-LEVEL TYPICAL WHITETAILS

YEARS	TOTAL NUMBER OF BUCKS	NUMBER IN 160–170	PERCENT IN 160–170	AVERAGE WORLD RECORD SCORE
1960–64	172	15	8.7	196 $^1/_8$
1965–69	181	18	9.9	200 $^3/_8$
1970–74	176	24	13.6	199 $^3/_8$
1975–79	196	32	16.3	190 $^4/_8$
1980–84	312	56	17.9	195 $^0/_8$
1985–89	578	149	25.8	197 $^0/_8$
1990–94	959	309	32.2	202 $^6/_8$
1995–99	1249	469	37.6	198 $^0/_8$
2000–04	1211	647	53.4	200 $^7/_8$

There are several important observations to be made from these figures, not the least of which is the dramatic increase since the mid-1980s in the total number of bucks being entered into the Boone and Crockett record book. This trend itself reflects several factors, one being that the actual number of deer in the woods has increased dramatically over the last 25 years, and another being the near-parallel increase in the actual number of hunters going into those woods. Even in those regions of the U.S. where hunter participation was declining, those people who did hunt were far more apt to drop a buck from the enlarged deer population. With that many more deer in the woodlands, there was also a dramatic increase in the availability of trophy-size bucks.

So what, you say? Well, consider this: Because of the shift downward in the overall median score, almost half the typical whitetail deer in the Boone and Crockett record book are under 170 inches, and the entry level is only 160 inches. This means that today there's only a measly 10 inches of difference between the entry level and the median score of the registered trophy whitetails. The other side of that amazing situation is found in the top half of the whitetail trophy population, the bucks that have antlers ranging from a little over 170 inches up to the incredible World Record typical whitetail score of 213 ⁵/₈ inches—the Hanson buck that was killed in Saskatchewan in 1991. The difference between the median and that one special buck is over *43 inches* of combined antler dimensions! What this all suggests is that the upper end of the age distribution is well-anchored, and the *potential* for longevity and large racks hasn't actually gone down; it's just that the overall median has shifted.

WHERE HAVE ALL THE NON-TYPICAL WHITETAILS GONE?

In the 1920s, more than half of all whitetail deer registered in the Boone and Crockett record books had non-typical antlers—they had tines that forked, grew in odd directions (including downward), were unsymmetrical, or were otherwise not typical of the basic "basket" shape of the classic whitetail. This percentage began to decline and since the 1970s, the percent of non-typical antlers has steadily decreased from over 40 percent to roughly a third of all whitetails registered at B&C. Strange! Over this same period, the non-typical racks also dropped the same 4 inches that the typical bucks did. The probable decline in bucks' ages could explain both the drop in score (as was shown earlier) and the lowered percentage of total deer. That's because whitetails and the other deer species generally don't begin to develop non-typical antlers

The tines on **typical** *whitetail antlers grow from the top surface of the main beams and extend upward. The Boone and Crockett Club scoring system determines the sum of beam and tine lengths, inside spread, and certain beam circumferences. Deviations from symmetry and the classic "basket" shape are penalized.*

Non-typical whitetail tines and points over 1 inch are included in the Boone and Crockett Club score regardless of their location or direction of growth. A lack of symmetry is penalized only for those tines that would be considered "typical." Consequently, the entry level and World Record scores are higher.

until late in life. Please understand, though, that I have no proof that a decline in age is involved here; it just provides a reasonable and plausible explanation.

WHAT'S HAPPENING TO THE NON-TYPICAL WHITETAILS?

YEARS	TYPICAL	NON-TYPICAL	TOTAL WHITETAILS	PERCENT NON-TYPICAL
1960–64	172	125	297	42.1
1965–69	181	120	301	39.9
1970–74	176	123	299	41.1
1975–79	196	124	320	38.8
1980–84	312	175	487	35.9
1985–89	578	313	891	35.1
1990–94	959	498	1457	34.2
1995–99	1249	637	1886	33.8
2000–04	1211	647	1858	34.8

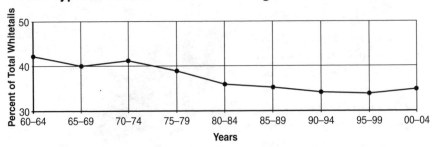

Non-Typical Whitetails as a Percentage of Total Whitetails

WHAT'S INFLUENCING THE NATURAL PRODUCTION OF ANTLERS?

We Antler People are approaching a fork in the road—a three-pronged fork, actually—and whether or not we happen to be deer hunters, the path we take will influence the availability of antlers for our collecting, crafting, and general enjoyment. Only about a third of the antler-obsessed people that I spoke with during the preparation for this book were active hunters. Hunters are organized to get what they want by the simple fact that their license purchases finance many government-controlled wildlife projects. In most states, hunters also have various organizations by which they are able to communicate their wishes for legislation and wildlife management. We Antler People, on the other hand, aren't organized at all; although the North American Shed Hunter's Club is a good start, we don't have a consumer advocacy group to represent us.

One thing for certain, though, is that the "antler mystique" has heated up to the extent that it is affecting wildlife management decisions . . . and not always in ways that would serve us well. Basically, most if not all of the various deer-management programs that strive to improve the herd through habitat improvement (or vice versa—to improve the habitat by controlling the potential damage done by deer), balanced doe/buck ratios, and slowed population growth are generally aimed at bucks growing larger antlers. Sometimes, though, it can be difficult to sort out what the official management goals really are: larger antlers for trophy hunters, or a quality hunting experience that honors the American tradition of meat-hunting?

Basically, there are three driving forces in North America that will affect the supply of antlers in the future:

1. Management of deer to produce larger antlers for exclusive trophy hunting ("the European model")

2. Management of deer to produce venison and preserve the tradition of hunting ("the American model")
3. Education of the public (especially schoolchildren) so that deer are seen to be a valuable but renewable resource

All three of these forces are manifested by official organizations or spokesmen and have in common the need for deer population control, the protection of wildlife habitat and valuable timber even if it means culling deer to achieve it, and the use of our natural interest in antlers as a carrot on a stick to get the job done. Let's take a closer look.

Managing Deer for Larger Antlers

The term "quality deer management" is often associated with the lowering of deer populations, with the production of larger antlers being a possible side benefit. A lot of good can come from that angle. But there's also a potential downside, and you never know for sure until you look closely whether "QDM" means management of deer for all of us or just for the production of trophy antlers for the elite few who can afford to exclude all others, as is the common practice in Europe even today. The Quality Deer Management Association (www.QDMA.com), an American organization, was primarily formed not to produce trophy bucks but to advise hunters about the benefits of reducing overpopulated whitetail herds on private lands. The QDMA originated in the South (particularly Texas) and Southeast and more recently has also been influential in northern Michigan—in all cases, areas where faulty management at some private hunting clubs had led to deer in poor physical condition with poorly formed antlers. Unfortunately, in a few regions of the United States, so-called "quality deer management" is now being independently advocated by some trophy hunters who misrepresent the facts regarding deer populations, overcrowding, and age ratios. Regardless of how "quality deer management" is actually applied in a given region, it appears that the professional wildlife managers within the state are often ignored or circumvented.

Currently, the QDMA helps educate landowners on how to improve their habitat by planting food plots and otherwise increasing those natural food supplies that are beneficial for antler development. Trophy hunters and landowners are also educated about the need for the selective shooting of does (female deer) so that a proper ratio of does to bucks is maintained. At its best, quality deer management offers some good solutions to several of the problems that deer present to our woodland habitats. This approach has, however, at its ugliest extreme the potential to exclude most of us from the woodlands . . . not just the ordinary hunter-sportsmen, but the shed-hunters, too, plus the bird-watchers and probably even the Boy Scouts. There's a fragile balance of intentions here. The tradition in Europe for many centuries has been that only the wealthy, privileged few had access to the hunting grounds. When deer are managed in America specifically for larger antlers, restrictions on access to private lands are based on the perceived need to protect the antlered bucks from the common man, so that only the paying customer may hunt them.

The "Alliance for Public Wildlife" was recently formed by U.S. and Canadian wildlife professionals to educate and alert the public regarding the current trend in North America toward the restrictive and exclusive systems now used in Europe. According to Keith McCaffery, who is himself an active spokesman for the Alliance, "Privatized deer management is not the best for wildlife in general because it is single-purpose with a limited ecological perspective. Too often, deer are farmed almost like cattle: they become a commodity where hobbies, profits, and markets tempt manipulation." If hunting were to be legislated out of existence in America, as it almost has been in England recently, then the "deer problem" ultimately would be solved by uniformed deer-executioners in helicopters and professional poisoners in the parks, and shed deer antlers would no longer be found on the ground in the spring woods. You think I'm kidding? Some years ago, New Zealand experienced an extreme surge in the population of their red deer, and in the absence of enough hunters to thin the herds, the job was done by wardens with helicopter-mounted machine guns.

At the state-government level, however, there are three other methods that wildlife managers have to limit the number of bucks that are killed so that they can grow larger antlers as they get older:

- Specifying a minimum antler size by imposing antler point restrictions (APRs)
- Reducing the number of days that bucks can be hunted
- Limiting the number of hunters who can harvest a buck (such as with the "party permits" that many states issue by lottery for doe-hunting)

There are some sharp divisions of opinion regarding whether managing deer for improved trophy hunting is entirely a good thing. Here are some of the issues that need to be confronted and resolved:

Loss of easy access to private lands. Currently, most hunters request permission to hunt private land and are usually granted access, the only "fees" required being respect of the land, perhaps a couple of venison steaks for the landowner, and maybe a thank-you note or a card at Christmastime. It's an American tradition. However, when landowners realize the potential of trophy management programs to produce profitable pay-to-hunt situations, the "No Trespassing" signs go up in order to protect the smaller bucks from being harvested. In the past two years, I personally have lost easy access to almost half of the land near where I live and hunt, all in the name of quality deer management. "Paid hunting" is the true name of "managing for large antlers" if the philosophy is taken to this point. Don't get me wrong here: I'm all for privatation and free enterprise, but don't forget—wild deer legally belong to the state, *not* to the landowner. If the deer on my own property are being lured past "No Trespassing" signs to greener, artificially cultivated pastures so that some other landowner can benefit financially from "our" deer, then there's not much "quality hunting" left for me to enjoy.

Loss of hunter acceptance by the non-hunting public. Most ordinary deer hunters such as myself tend to admire the trophy hunters for their skill and perseverance, but the non-hunting public tends to scorn those who would kill a trophy animal mostly for its value as a display item. On the other hand, the ordinary deer hunter is perceived by most non-hunters to be someone who eats the venison he obtains while helping to keep the deer herd under control, off the roads, and out of their lawns.

Antler Point Restrictions. APRs at the state level present a potentially kinder, gentler version of QDM that tends to fall short of the pay-to-hunt options, and it's one that might be most beneficial in the long run to shed-hunters. This system of deer management requires that hunters refrain from shooting any buck that has fewer points (tines) than are specified. For example, the APR program recently installed in Pennsylvania stipulates that in certain areas of the state, a buck must have four points to be legal game; in other areas, it must have at least three points on one of its antlers. The intent here is to let one full generation of yearling bucks live another year so that they can develop larger antlers. Furthermore, the buck population is increased theoretically for the following year and in subsequent years.

Having a more huntable deer population helps Pennsylvania to continue drawing the many thousands of people who travel there every year for "deer camp." After the first couple of years, APR programs are generally good for the local economy and good for the supply of natural foods—assuming that when hunters have to pass on a buck, they'll be more inclined to harvest a surplus doe instead. Other states are experimenting with APRs in limited areas, and Mississippi and Arkansas have already adopted it statewide.

However, APRs were being applied in the western states on elk and mule deer way back in the early twentieth century, but the system was dropped largely because it could not be shown to be effective in producing larger antlers, and because so many accidental illegal kills were occurring. And there are, of course, also some new problems associated with the current APR systems. For one thing, it's not simple arithmetic that the young bucks that were protected will result in a corresponding increase in the total number of bucks next year. No, not by a long shot. That's because the reduction of females that is necessary to accommodate more bucks in the herd actually results in fewer buck fawns in the spring. In other words, because the birthrates for male and female fawns is very close to one-to-one, the removal of one adult doe (as an intended substitute for harvesting a young buck) actually results in one less buck fawn born in the spring. And if you project that outcome to the following year, there will be one less buck yearling in the very age class that the APR system is supposed to be protecting.

But there's worse news: studies show that in the long run, APRs can reduce the genetic potential for large antlers. This works on the principle that all bucks do not have the same ability to produce large antlers in their progeny. In most regions, a $1\frac{1}{2}$-year-old buck is typically a two-pointed "spike" or a four-pointed "fork horn," but in mineral-and-calorie-rich farmlands, a yearling will average between five and six points. Wisconsin's Keith McCaffery has seen a yearling buck with 14 points that scored 142 inches on the Boone and Crockett system. So, under the APR system, those young bucks that are genetically superior in their potential to grow antlers would be most likely to be mistaken for older deer and targeted, leaving only the smaller-racked bucks. These studies have further shown statistically that when more than half of yearling bucks are removed in this way from the gene pool, the genetics of the herds will swing toward smaller antlers.

In the long run, is the Antler Point Restriction program a good thing or a bad thing? And what's the picky difference between APR programs and "quality deer management" for antlers? Do they both bring us too close to the pay-to-hunt model, or will we be finding so many more and bigger shed antlers in the future that we won't care what it costs to take a walk in the woods? At this time, we don't know. Time will tell.

Managing Deer for Venison and Preserving Tradition

Most of the quality deer management programs are centered around antler development in one way or another. Antlers are often used to keep citizens interested, even when the goals may include other developments. Try for a moment to imagine it being any other way—a world without antlers. (This won't be an easy exercise for an antler fanatic!) If you need help here, try thinking about how each year in the Ozarks, rural people used to go out into the woodlands to harvest feral hogs (which had grown big on wild herbs, berries, and acorns), and then smoke the pork over hickory embers. The next spring, they'd let a new batch of piglets go off into the woods to forage for themselves and go wild until the next butchering season came around. In some ways our deer hunting is like that: a tradition that places richly flavored meat on the supper table. It's only when antlers become more important than venison that the picture begins to go out of focus.

The current management-for-venison programs can actually work to the advantage of we Antler People. These programs are, frankly, the way things are right now in most of the states—the good old days of traditional deer hunting are still here. Even in Pennsylvania and the other states where APRs are being applied for the first time, the emphasis is still on hunter satisfaction ("Please, one more shot . . ."), since hunting is also where the money comes from.

Hunters support conservation more enthusiastically and with more money than any other interest group. The American tradition of being able to hunt regardless of our race, color, creed, tax bracket, or SUV model continues to drive the continued production of antlers and venison for all of us. It's the active participation of hunters voting with their dollars that supports the professional and responsible management of deer. Ultimately, it is the hunter organizations that push for limits and self-regulation. What all of this contributes to antler production includes the easy access for shed-hunting and an ongoing supply of antlers to collect and mount.

Education of the Public

Try picking up a single antler with your mind at ease, maybe even with your eyes closed. Wherever you grasp, it gently urges you to let it rotate to a position of perfect balance around a center of gravity somewhere in the empty space framed by the curves of the tines and beam. Change your grip, and it happens again—the antler feels alive. Dean Ziegler, founder of the National Whitetail Deer Education Foundation, believes our continued human contact with antlers as tools and implements, from the Paleolithic Era down to recent history, has become ingrained within our culture, perhaps even our genetic heritage. Kids, he says, are fascinated by antlers. When an antler is first shown to a fifth-grade class,

*The "Dinosaur"
of Deerassic Park
(www.deerassicpark.com),
one of many deer that
can be seen there in a
natural setting.*

the room suddenly goes silent. All eyes focus on the instructor. When the antler is handed to the kid in the first row to be passed around . . . it stays right there—the kid wants to keep it. Anything else being passed around, such as a buckeye chestnut or a quartz rock, goes around the room in no time at all. The antler is finally handed along—slowly, reluctantly—and wherever it happens to be in the classroom, the kids nearest to it aren't paying attention to the instructor any more.

Education is the third part in that fork in the road I told you about—the road determining the future of antlers. The first part I described was the trend toward the management of deer for the singular purpose of antler development. (Deer biologist Keith McCaffery calls it "horn porn.") The second prong, the one in the middle, is a continuation of the current American-style management philosophy of maintaining a "controlled abundance" with reasonable access to the woodlands for everyone, including non-hunters. The third prong, education, answers our need to reconnect to youth and the outdoors, and therein lies the future of antlers . . . and perhaps our own future as well.

I first heard about Dean Ziegler's whitetail education programs from Jack Brown, the "Bonecarver" of eBay fame. Jack had been commissioned by Ziegler to carve a pair of trophy whitetail antlers into a "Dueling Dragons" sculpture for a drawing at a 2004 fundraiser for "Deerassic Park." Yes, there really is a place with the unlikely name of Deerassic Park. (Sounds like *Jurassic Park*, the dinosaur movie . . . get it?) It's a work under development in southeastern Ohio, a 117-acre wooded area where Ziegler has headquartered the education programs

Jodi Kellar, program director of the National Whitetail Deer Education Foundation, holds one of several antlers that are shown to school children as part of an extensive program to reconnect children to the outdoors and nature.

and administrative staff of the National Whitetail Deer Education Foundation. It features a deer farm, a rustic camping area, and a huge pavilion with a parking lot. Soon there will also be a museum to house the Ohio Whitetail Hall of Fame, consisting initially of all the antlers that Ziegler has been collecting since the 1970s, which are absolutely fantastic.

The Bonecarver had told me, "You won't believe this place!" and he was right. I didn't. I had to see it for myself, and as a result of going there to spend the weekend, I'm convinced that the future of both American-style deer hunting and a continued reverence for deer and their antlers among non-hunters depends on the success of education programs such as those I found there. One of the programs is named "The Outside Is IN!"—meaning "in fashion" or "in vogue" or, as the kids themselves often say when handling a shed antler or solving a predator-prey riddle while sitting on a deerskin, "Cool!"

One popular activity involves the children acting out the dynamics of rapid deer population growth as one becomes two, two become four, four become eight, and so on, with all this being played against a dwindling "food supply"—sometimes just rocks in a bucket. At the point that this fast-paced game breaks down because of mock overpopulation, the instructor gently makes the point that in the absence of natural predators such as wolves and cougars, help from human hunters is needed to keep deer populations in balance and harmony with all the other creatures of nature. From there, several other examples of how organisms interact with each other are demonstrated, and then the subject evolves painlessly into social studies and history lessons, which in turn opens the door to instruction on how humans (and deer) are affecting the physical environment.

Programs like this funnel the natural fascination that kids have for antlers into a more comprehensive appreciation of how deer fit into the ecosystem. There are programs specifically designed for different grade levels, including more sophisticated presentations for high school and college students. The programs follow Ohio's academic content standards, and they're available to schools at cost (and free when necessary), which is particularly helpful in this age of continuing budget cuts. There are currently fifteen paid instructors who make presentations in the school classrooms, and a smaller resident staff for field trips to Deerassic Park, where the children can view the deer and experience hands-on the wonders of the woods. At one point during a "walk on the wild side," the group is invited to sit down wherever they wish and be quiet for three minutes. When that time is up, many of the children appear to be more focused on the woods than before. Often the boisterous ones fall silent, and the shy children begin asking questions.

So, who's paying for all this? That's a story in itself. . . . The driving force and sustaining energy behind Deerassic Park and the Education Foundation is Dean Ziegler. He began collecting whitetail antlers while working as a taxidermist, and when he took his remarkable collection (the "Whitetail Spectacular") on the road in a walk-through trailer, he ran into more people interested in antlers than even he thought were out there. He founded the NWDEF in 1996 and later acquired the Deerassic Park property, and this is where the unique "Deerassic Classic Giveaway" has been held every August since 2003. Ten thousand $100 raffle tickets are sold, and there are over 250 prizes. At the 2005 Classic, the prizes included 78 rifles and shotguns, six 4WD vehicles, 11 ATVs, 15 vacation packages, two Harleys, seven big-screen televisions, two boats, and over 120 *other* similar prizes, all good stuff that anyone

Dean Ziegler, the widely known whitetail deer expert who organized the National Whitetail Deer Education Foundation and had the vision to develop Deerassic Park, holds antlers shed by "Dinosaur," a prime example of a non-typical whitetail buck.

would want to take home, especially the grand prize of $50,000 in cold, hard cash. Winning numbers are announced every minute and forty-five seconds for six solid hours. It's a picnic, all right, and everyone is happy and smiling because they're all just one more minute or two away from maybe winning something. (Multiple winnings can occur on a single ticket.) Of course, there probably are some folks who would consider all this to be "shameless exploitation" of the noble whitetail deer. But it doesn't feel that way to me, especially when I consider how the money is being used and when I think of the kids who get to hold an antler, many of them for the first time ever.

As Ziegler and I sat on the porch of the log cabin that also serves as an office, I asked him what he thought of the various deer management philosophies now being applied. He didn't answer that question directly, but he offered some thoughts. The most important thing, he said, is that the genetics that control antler development need to be defined by actual competition between truly adult bucks. The larger-antlered bucks usually win the right to breed, and this situation is best accomplished when a natural ratio of one-to-one bucks and does exists. Antler point restrictions probably would work the best if they were set to protect the bigger bucks, not the small ones, because it's when bucks reach age 3 $1/2$ that the serious head-butting contests for genetic supremacy begin in earnest. He told me then about a 1 $1/2$-year-old buck on his game farm that had grown full-size antlers that scored an amazing 140 inches, proving that if the genes are there, the antlers can be too.

The most extreme but also most effective way to manage whitetails for antlers, Ziegler said, would be to completely close the season on all bucks for about four years. That would allow four different age groups of bucks to slug it out and the antler genes would probably be improved. But you try something like that and you won't have any friends for a long time! Besides, a whole four years' worth of young teenagers who would have become deer hunters would be lost to us, and we need them. One other way that would be almost as effective and almost as unpopular would be restricting a hunter to harvesting only one buck every four years, although he could pick when the year was going to be when he saw the buck he was after—in other words, he could hunt for up to four years for bucks, but knowing that he'd lose his right to shoot another one until the next period, he certainly wouldn't blow it all on a small-antlered buck. Instead, he'd more likely wait for the Big One and maybe even have more fun doing it that way.

That's what Ziegler told me, and it makes a lot of sense. By exercising self-restraint on virtually all bucks except for the wall-hangers, we could hunt that expanding population of trophy-antlered bucks (and their springtime shed antlers) as though we had joined the exclusive quality-deer-management group. But we could do it all American-style without having to lose access to private property or having to pay the prohibitive European-model fees. We could feel like nobles and hunt like pioneers.

THE CANARY IN THE COAL MINE

Years ago, coal miners brought caged canaries into the mines to warn them of rising levels of deadly but scentless gases such as carbon monoxide. The bright song in the dark gloom surely was reassuring to hear, but if the delicate bird fell dead, it was time to go somewhere else very quickly. I think that in some ways, the antlers of whitetails, mule deer, moose, caribou, and elk serve us as harbingers of an approaching future—not just as indicators of ecological health on several levels, which they are, but also as lightning rods of sorts that ground our fascination with a wild world that we're otherwise mostly unable to touch and hold. I once read a science-fiction story in which aliens gained hypnotic control over humans just by supplying them with special "worry stones" to hold. I often think of that story when I hand an antler to someone; they explore its curves and surface textures more with their hands than their eyes. This intense, growing interest in antlers that has developed at the turn of the twenty-first century possibly indicates the beginning of humans understanding their relationship with nature on a spiritual plane.

Or maybe it's just a happy consequence of the unavailability of elephant ivory, the advantages of Internet commerce and communication, and an expanding deer population. As we've seen, antlers mean different things to different people: the artist-carver looks at an antler differently than a weekend hunter does, and a shed-hunter prizes a humble spike antler in ways that a trophy collector cannot begin to comprehend. You might ask yourself what antlers mean to you personally . . . and I'll bet that you'll struggle to come up with a tangible answer in twenty-five words or less that doesn't get garbled in a fog of metaphysics.

And by the way, don't ask me to help you. Before I began to write this book I thought that I already knew why antlers fascinated me. Now, here at the end, supposedly enlightened by the knowledge I have gained along the way, I find that even the answer with which I began now eludes me. In fact, I'm completely mystified. But the canary is still singing.

APPENDIX

BOONE AND CROCKETT SCORE SHEETS

Records of
North American
Big Game

250 Station Drive
Missoula, MT 59801
(406) 542-1888

BOONE AND CROCKETT CLUB®
OFFICIAL SCORING SYSTEM FOR NORTH AMERICAN BIG GAME TROPHIES

MINIMUM SCORES

	AWARDS	ALL-TIME
whitetail	160	170
Coues'	100	110

TYPICAL
WHITETAIL AND COUES' DEER

KIND OF DEER (check one)
☐ whitetail
☐ Coues'

Detail of Point
Measurement

Abnormal Points	
Right Antler	Left Antler
SUBTOTALS	
TOTAL TO E	

SEE OTHER SIDE FOR INSTRUCTIONS		COLUMN 1	COLUMN 2	COLUMN 3	COLUMN 4
A. No. Points on Right Antler	No. Points on Left Antler	Spread Credit	Right Antler	Left Antler	Difference
B. Tip to Tip Spread	C. Greatest Spread				
D. Inside Spread of Main Beams	SPREAD CREDIT MAY EQUAL BUT NOT EXCEED LONGER MAIN BEAM				
E. Total of Lengths of Abnormal Points					
F. Length of Main Beam					
G-1. Length of First Point					
G-2. Length of Second Point					
G-3. Length of Third Point					
G-4. Length of Fourth Point, If Present					
G-5. Length of Fifth Point, If Present					
G-6. Length of Sixth Point, If Present					
G-7. Length of Seventh Point, If Present					
H-1. Circumference at Smallest Place Between Burr and First Point					
H-2. Circumference at Smallest Place Between First and Second Points					
H-3. Circumference at Smallest Place Between Second and Third Points					
H-4. Circumference at Smallest Place Between Third and Fourth Points					
	TOTALS				

ADD	Column 1		Exact Locality Where Killed:	
	Column 2		Date Killed:	Hunter:
	Column 3		Owner:	Telephone #:
	Subtotal		Owner's Address:	
SUBTRACT Column 4			Guide's Name and Address:	
FINAL SCORE			Remarks: (Mention Any Abnormalities or Unique Qualities)	OM I.D. Number

I, _____ , certify that I have measured this trophy on _____
PRINT NAME   MM/DD/YYYYY

at _____
STREET ADDRESS   CITY   STATE/PROVINCE

and that these measurements and data are, to the best of my knowledge and belief, made in accordance with the instructions given.

Witness: _____ Signature: _____ I.D. Number ☐☐☐☐
                               B&C OFFICIAL MEASURER

INSTRUCTIONS FOR MEASURING TYPICAL WHITETAIL AND COUES' DEER

All measurements must be made with a 1/4-inch wide flexible steel tape to the nearest one-eighth of an inch. (Note: A flexible steel cable can be used to measure points and main beams only.) Enter fractional figures in eighths, without reduction. Official measurements cannot be taken until the antlers have air dried for at least 60 days after the animal was killed.

  A. Number of Points on Each Antler: To be counted a point, the projection must be at least one inch long, with the length exceeding width at one inch or more of length. All points are measured from tip of point to nearest edge of beam as illustrated. Beam tip is counted as a point but not measured as a point.

  B. Tip to Tip Spread is measured between tips of main beams.

  C. Greatest Spread is measured between perpendiculars at a right angle to the center line of the skull at widest part, whether across main beams or points.

  D. Inside Spread of Main Beams is measured at a right angle to the center line of the skull at widest point between main beams. Enter this measurement again as the Spread Credit if it is less than or equal to the length of the longer main beam; if greater, enter longer main beam length for Spread Credit.

  E. Total of Lengths of all Abnormal Points: Abnormal Points are those non-typical in location (such as points originating from a point or from bottom or sides of main beam) or extra points beyond the normal pattern of points. Measure in usual manner and enter in appropriate blanks.

  F. Length of Main Beam is measured from the center of the lowest outside edge of burr over the outer side to the most distant point of the main beam. The point of beginning is that point on the burr where the center line along the outer side of the beam intersects the burr, then following generally the line of the illustration.

  G-1-2-3-4-5-6-7. Length of Normal Points: Normal points project from the top of the main beam. They are measured from nearest edge of main beam over outer curve to tip. Lay the tape along the outer curve of the beam so that the top edge of the tape coincides with the top edge of the beam on both sides of the point to determine the baseline for point measurements. Record point lengths in appropriate blanks.

  H-1-2-3-4. Circumferences are taken as detailed in illustration for each measurement. If brow point is missing, take H-1 and H-2 at smallest place between burr and G-2. If G-4 is missing, take H-4 halfway between G-3 and tip of main beam.

ENTRY AFFIDAVIT FOR ALL HUNTER-TAKEN TROPHIES

For the purpose of entry into the Boone and Crockett Club's® records, North American big game harvested by the use of the following methods or under the following conditions are ineligible:

  I. Spotting or herding game from the air, followed by landing in its vicinity for the purpose of pursuit and shooting;

  II. Herding or chasing with the aid of any motorized equipment;

  III. Use of electronic communication devices, artificial lighting, or electronic light intensifying devices;

  IV. Confined by artificial barriers, including escape-proof fenced enclosures;

  V. Transplanted for the purpose of commercial shooting;

  VI. By the use of traps or pharmaceuticals;

  VII. While swimming, helpless in deep snow, or helpless in any other natural or artificial medium;

  VIII. On another hunter's license;

  IX. Not in full compliance with the game laws or regulations of the federal government or of any state, province, territory, or tribal council on reservations or tribal lands;

I certify that the trophy scored on this chart was not taken in violation of the conditions listed above. In signing this statement, I understand that if the information provided on this entry is found to be misrepresented or fraudulent in any respect, it will not be accepted into the Awards Program and 1) all of my prior entries are subject to deletion from future editions of **Records of North American Big Game** 2) future entries may not be accepted.

FAIR CHASE, as defined by the Boone and Crockett Club®, is the ethical, sportsmanlike and lawful pursuit and taking of any free-ranging wild, native North American big game animal in a manner that does not give the hunter an improper advantage over such game animals.

The Boone and Crockett Club® may exclude the entry of any animal that it deems to have been taken in an unethical manner or under conditions deemed inappropriate by the Club.

Date: _____ Signature of Hunter: _____
                         (SIGNATURE MUST BE WITNESSED BY AN OFFICIAL MEASURER OR A NOTARY PUBLIC.)

Date: _____ Signature of Notary or Official Measurer: _____

Records of
North American
Big Game

250 Station Drive
Missoula, MT 59801
(406) 542-1888

BOONE AND CROCKETT CLUB®
OFFICIAL SCORING SYSTEM FOR NORTH AMERICAN BIG GAME TROPHIES

NON-TYPICAL
WHITETAIL AND COUES' DEER

MINIMUM SCORES		
	AWARDS	ALL-TIME
whitetail	185	195
Coues'	105	120

KIND OF DEER (check one)
☐ whitetail
☐ Coues'

Abnormal Points	
Right Antler	Left Antler

G2 G3 G4 G5 G6 E E H4 H3 G1 E F H2 H1 B C D

Detail of Point Measurement

SUBTOTALS		
E. TOTAL		

SEE OTHER SIDE FOR INSTRUCTIONS				COLUMN 1	COLUMN 2	COLUMN 3	COLUMN 4
A. No. Points on Right Antler		No. Points on Left Antler		Spread Credit	Right Antler	Left Antler	Difference
B. Tip to Tip Spread		C. Greatest Spread					
D. Inside Spread of Main Beams		SPREAD CREDIT MAY EQUAL BUT NOT EXCEED LONGER MAIN BEAM					
F. Length of Main Beam							
G-1. Length of First Point							
G-2. Length of Second Point							
G-3. Length of Third Point							
G-4. Length of Fourth Point, If Present							
G-5. Length of Fifth Point, If Present							
G-6. Length of Sixth Point, If Present							
G-7. Length of Seventh Point, If Present							
H-1. Circumference at Smallest Place Between Burr and First Point							
H-2. Circumference at Smallest Place Between First and Second Points							
H-3. Circumference at Smallest Place Between Second and Third Points							
H-4. Circumference at Smallest Place Between Third and Fourth Points							
			TOTALS				

ADD	Column 1		Exact Locality Where Killed:	
	Column 2		Date Killed:	Hunter:
	Column 3		Owner:	Telephone #:
	Subtotal		Owner's Address:	
SUBTRACT Column 4			Guide's Name and Address:	
	Subtotal		Remarks: (Mention Any Abnormalities or Unique Qualities)	
ADD Line E Total				
FINAL SCORE				OM I.D. Number

I, _____ , certify that I have measured this trophy on _____
PRINT NAME   MM/DD/YYYYY

at _____
STREET ADDRESS   CITY   STATE/PROVINCE

and that these measurements and data are, to the best of my knowledge and belief, made in accordance with the instructions given.

Witness: _____ Signature: _____ I.D. Number
                                              B&C OFFICIAL MEASURER

INSTRUCTIONS FOR MEASURING NON-TYPICAL WHITETAIL AND COUES' DEER

All measurements must be made with a 1/4-inch wide flexible steel tape to the nearest one-eighth of an inch. (Note: A flexible steel cable can be used to measure points and main beams only.) Enter fractional figures in eighths, without reduction. Official measurements cannot be taken until the antlers have air dried for at least 60 days after the animal was killed.

A. Number of Points on Each Antler: To be counted a point, the projection must be at least one inch long, with the length exceeding width at one inch or more of length. All points are measured from tip of point to nearest edge of beam as illustrated. Beam tip is counted as a point but not measured as a point.

B. Tip to Tip Spread is measured between tips of main beams.

C. Greatest Spread is measured between perpendiculars at a right angle to the center line of the skull at widest part, whether across main beams or points.

D. Inside Spread of Main Beams is measured at a right angle to the center line of the skull at widest point between main beams. Enter this measurement again as the Spread Credit if it is less than or equal to the length of the longer main beam; if greater, enter longer main beam length for Spread Credit.

E. Total of Lengths of all Abnormal Points: Abnormal Points are those non-typical in location (such as points originating from a point or from bottom or sides of main beam) or extra points beyond the normal pattern of points. Measure in usual manner and enter in appropriate blanks.

F. Length of Main Beam is measured from the center of the lowest outside edge of burr over the outer side to the most distant point of the main beam. The point of beginning is that point on the burr where the center line along the outer side of the beam intersects the burr, then following generally the line of the illustration.

G-1-2-3-4-5-6-7. Length of Normal Points: Normal points project from the top of the main beam. They are measured from nearest edge of main beam over outer curve to tip. Lay the tape along the outer curve of the beam so that the top edge of the tape coincides with the top edge of the beam on both sides of the point to determine the baseline for point measurement. Record point lengths in appropriate blanks.

H-1-2-3-4. Circumferences are taken as detailed in illustration for each measurement. If brow point is missing, take H-1 and H-2 at smallest place between burr and G-2. If G-4 is missing, take H-4 halfway between G-3 and tip of main beam.

ENTRY AFFIDAVIT FOR ALL HUNTER-TAKEN TROPHIES

For the purpose of entry into the Boone and Crockett Club's® records, North American big game harvested by the use of the following methods or under the following conditions are ineligible:

   I.   Spotting or herding game from the air, followed by landing in its vicinity for the purpose of pursuit and shooting;
   II. Herding or chasing with the aid of any motorized equipment;
   III. Use of electronic communication devices, artificial lighting, or electronic light intensifying devices;
   IV. Confined by artificial barriers, including escape-proof fenced enclosures;
   V.   Transplanted for the purpose of commercial shooting;
   VI. By the use of traps or pharmaceuticals;
   VII. While swimming, helpless in deep snow, or helpless in any other natural or artificial medium;
   VIII. On another hunter's license;
   IX. Not in full compliance with the game laws or regulations of the federal government or of any state, province, territory, or tribal council on reservations or tribal lands;

I certify that the trophy scored on this chart was not taken in violation of the conditions listed above. In signing this statement, I understand that if the information provided on this entry is found to be misrepresented or fraudulent in any respect, it will not be accepted into the Awards Program and 1) all of my prior entries are subject to deletion from future editions of **Records of North American Big Game** 2) future entries may not be accepted.

FAIR CHASE, as defined by the Boone and Crockett Club®, is the ethical, sportsmanlike and lawful pursuit and taking of any free-ranging wild, native North American big game animal in a manner that does not give the hunter an improper advantage over such game animals.

The Boone and Crockett Club® may exclude the entry of any animal that it deems to have been taken in an unethical manner or under conditions deemed inappropriate by the Club.

Date: _____ Signature of Hunter: _____
                                              (SIGNATURE MUST BE WITNESSED BY AN OFFICIAL MEASURER OR A NOTARY PUBLIC.)

Date: _____ Signature of Notary or Official Measurer: _____

Records of
North American
Big Game

250 Station Drive
Missoula, MT 59801
(406) 542-1888

BOONE AND CROCKETT CLUB®
OFFICIAL SCORING SYSTEM FOR NORTH AMERICAN BIG GAME TROPHIES

TYPICAL
MULE DEER AND BLACKTAIL DEER

MINIMUM SCORES	AWARDS	ALL-TIME
mule deer	180	190
Columbia blacktail	125	135
Sitka blacktail	100	108

KIND OF DEER (check one)
- ☐ mule deer
- ☐ Columbia blacktail
- ☐ Sitka blacktail

Detail of Point Measurement

Abnormal Points	
Right Antler	Left Antler

SUBTOTALS	
TOTAL TO E	

SEE OTHER SIDE FOR INSTRUCTIONS

		COLUMN 1	COLUMN 2	COLUMN 3	COLUMN 4
A. No. Points on Right Antler	No. Points on Left Antler	Spread Credit	Right Antler	Left Antler	Difference
B. Tip to Tip Spread	C. Greatest Spread				
D. Inside Spread of Main Beams	SPREAD CREDIT MAY EQUAL BUT NOT EXCEED LONGER MAIN BEAM				
E. Total of Lengths of Abnormal Points					
F. Length of Main Beam					
G-1. Length of First Point, If Present					
G-2. Length of Second Point					
G-3. Length of Third Point, If Present					
G-4. Length of Fourth Point, If Present					
H-1. Circumference at Smallest Place Between Burr and First Point					
H-2. Circumference at Smallest Place Between First and Second Points					
H-3. Circumference at Smallest Place Between Main Beam and Third Point					
H-4. Circumference at Smallest Place Between Second and Fourth Points					
TOTALS					

ADD	Column 1		Exact Locality Where Killed:
	Column 2		Date Killed: Hunter:
	Column 3		Owner: Telephone #:
	Subtotal		Owner's Address:
SUBTRACT Column 4			Guide's Name and Address:
FINAL SCORE			Remarks: (Mention Any Abnormalities or Unique Qualities)

OM I.D. Number

I, _____, certify that I have measured this trophy on _____
              PRINT NAME   MM/DD/YYYYY

at _____
          STREET ADDRESS   CITY   STATE/PROVINCE

and that these measurements and data are, to the best of my knowledge and belief, made in accordance with the instructions given.

Witness: _____ Signature: _____ I.D. Number [ ][ ][ ][ ]
                                                          B&C OFFICIAL MEASURER

INSTRUCTIONS FOR MEASURING TYPICAL MULE AND BLACKTAIL DEER

All measurements must be made with a 1/4-inch wide flexible steel tape to the nearest one-eighth of an inch. (Note: A flexible steel cable can be used to measure points and main beams only.) Enter fractional figures in eighths, without reduction. Official measurements cannot be taken until the antlers have air dried for at least 60 days after the animal was killed.

A. Number of Points on Each Antler: To be counted a point, the projection must be at least one inch long, with length exceeding width at one inch or more of length. All points are measured from tip of point to nearest edge of beam. Beam tip is counted as a point but not measured as a point.

B. Tip to Tip Spread is measured between tips of main beams.

C. Greatest Spread is measured between perpendiculars at a right angle to the center line of the skull at widest part, whether across main beams or points.

D. Inside Spread of Main Beams is measured at a right angle to the center line of the skull at widest point between main beams. Enter this measurement again as the Spread Credit **if** it is less than or equal to the length of the longer main beam; if greater, enter longer main beam length for Spread Credit.

E. Total of Lengths of all Abnormal Points: Abnormal Points are those non-typical in location such as points originating from a point (exception: G-3 originates from G-2 in perfectly normal fashion) or from bottom or sides of main beam, or any points beyond the normal pattern of five (including beam tip) per antler. Measure each abnormal point in usual manner and enter in appropriate blanks.

F. Length of Main Beam is measured from the center of the lowest outside edge of burr over the outer side to the most distant point of the Main Beam. The point of beginning is that point on the burr where the center line along the outer side of the beam intersects the burr, then following generally the line of the illustration.

G-1-2-3-4. Length of Normal Points: Normal points are the brow tines and the upper and lower forks as shown in the illustration. They are measured from nearest edge of main beam over outer curve to tip. Lay the tape along the outer curve of the beam so that the top edge of the tape coincides with the top edge of the beam on both sides of point to determine the baseline for point measurement. Record point lengths in appropriate blanks.

H-1-2-3-4. Circumferences are taken as detailed in illustration for each measurement. If brow point is missing, take H-1 and H-2 at smallest place between burr and G-2. If G-3 is missing, take H-3 halfway between the base and tip of G-2. If G-4 is missing, take H-4 halfway between G-2 and tip of main beam.

ENTRY AFFIDAVIT FOR ALL HUNTER-TAKEN TROPHIES

For the purpose of entry into the Boone and Crockett Club's® records, North American big game harvested by the use of the following methods or under the following conditions are ineligible:

   I.   Spotting or herding game from the air, followed by landing in its vicinity for the purpose of pursuit and shooting;
   II. Herding or chasing with the aid of any motorized equipment;
   III. Use of electronic communication devices, artificial lighting, or electronic light intensifying devices;
   IV. Confined by artificial barriers, including escape-proof fenced enclosures;
   V.   Transplanted for the purpose of commercial shooting;
   VI. By the use of traps or pharmaceuticals;
   VII. While swimming, helpless in deep snow, or helpless in any other natural or artificial medium;
   VIII. On another hunter's license;
   IX. Not in full compliance with the game laws or regulations of the federal government or of any state, province, territory, or tribal council on reservations or tribal lands;

I certify that the trophy scored on this chart was not taken in violation of the conditions listed above. In signing this statement, I understand that if the information provided on this entry is found to be misrepresented or fraudulent in any respect, it will not be accepted into the Awards Program and 1) all of my prior entries are subject to deletion from future editions of **Records of North American Big Game** 2) future entries may not be accepted.

FAIR CHASE, as defined by the Boone and Crockett Club®, is the ethical, sportsmanlike and lawful pursuit and taking of any free-ranging wild, native North American big game animal in a manner that does not give the hunter an improper advantage over such game animals.

The Boone and Crockett Club® may exclude the entry of any animal that it deems to have been taken in an unethical manner or under conditions deemed inappropriate by the Club.

Date: _____ Signature of Hunter: _____
                                                  (SIGNATURE MUST BE WITNESSED BY AN OFFICIAL MEASURER OR A NOTARY PUBLIC.)

Date: _____ Signature of Notary or Official Measurer: _____

Records of
North American
Big Game

250 Station Drive
Missoula, MT 59801
(406) 542-1888

BOONE AND CROCKETT CLUB®
OFFICIAL SCORING SYSTEM FOR NORTH AMERICAN BIG GAME TROPHIES

	MINIMUM SCORES	
	AWARDS	ALL-TIME
mule deer	215	230
Columbia blacktail	155	155
Sitka blacktail	118	118

NON-TYPICAL
MULE DEER AND BLACKTAIL DEER

Abnormal Points	
Right Antler	Left Antler

Detail of Point Measurement

SUBTOTALS	
E. TOTAL	

SEE OTHER SIDE FOR INSTRUCTIONS

			COLUMN 1	COLUMN 2	COLUMN 3	COLUMN 4
A. No. Points on Right Antler		No. Points on Left Antler	Spread Credit	Right Antler	Left Antler	Difference
B. Tip to Tip Spread		C. Greatest Spread				
D. Inside Spread of Main Beams		SPREAD CREDIT MAY EQUAL BUT NOT EXCEED LONGER MAIN BEAM				
F. Length of Main Beam						
G-1. Length of First Point, If Present						
G-2. Length of Second Point						
G-3. Length of Third Point, If Present						
G-4. Length of Fourth Point, If Present						
H-1. Circumference at Smallest Place Between Burr and First Point						
H-2. Circumference at Smallest Place Between First and Second Points						
H-3. Circumference at Smallest Place Between Main Beam and Third Point						
H-4. Circumference at Smallest Place Between Second and Fourth Points						
		TOTALS				

ADD	Column 1		Exact Locality Where Killed:	
	Column 2		Date Killed:	Hunter:
	Column 3		Owner:	Telephone #:
	Subtotal		Owner's Address:	
SUBTRACT Column 4			Guide's Name and Address:	
	Subtotal		Remarks: (Mention Any Abnormalities or Unique Qualities)	
	ADD Line E Total			
FINAL SCORE				

OM I.D. Number

I, _____ , certify that I have measured this trophy on _____
   PRINT NAME   MM/DD/YYYYY

at _____
   STREET ADDRESS   CITY   STATE/PROVINCE

and that these measurements and data are, to the best of my knowledge and belief, made in accordance with the instructions given.

Witness: _____ Signature:_____ I.D. Number ☐ ☐ ☐ ☐
                                                              B&C OFFICIAL MEASURER

INSTRUCTIONS FOR MEASURING NON-TYPICAL MULE DEER AND BLACKTAIL

All measurements must be made with a 1/4-inch wide flexible steel tape to the nearest one-eighth of an inch. (Note: A flexible steel cable can be used to measure points and main beams only.) Enter fractional figures in eighths, without reduction. Official measurements cannot be taken until the antlers have air dried for at least 60 days after the animal was killed.

A. Number of Points on Each Antler: To be counted a point, the projection must be at least one inch long, with length exceeding width at one inch or more of length. All points are measured from tip of point to nearest edge of beam as illustrated. Beam tip is counted as a point but not measured as a point.

B. Tip to Tip Spread is measured between tips of main beams.

C. Greatest Spread is measured between perpendiculars at a right angle to the center line of the skull at widest part, whether across main beams or points.

D. Inside Spread of Main Beams is measured at a right angle to the center line of the skull at widest point between main beams. Enter this measurement again as the Spread Credit if it is less than or equal to the length of the longer main beam; if greater, enter longer main beam length for Spread Credit.

E. Total of Lengths of all Abnormal Points: Abnormal Points are those non-typical in location such as points originating from a point (exception: G-3 originates from G-2 in perfectly normal fashion) or from bottom or sides of main beam, or any points beyond the normal pattern of five (including beam tip) per antler. Measure each abnormal point in usual manner and enter in appropriate blanks.

F. Length of Main Beam is measured from the center of the lowest outside edge of burr over the outer side to the most distant point of the main beam. The point of beginning is that point on the burr where the center line along the outer side of the beam intersects the burr, then following generally the line of the illustration.

G-1-2-3-4. Length of Normal Points: Normal points are the brow tines and the upper and lower forks as shown in the illustration. They are measured from nearest edge of main beam over outer curve to tip. Lay the tape along the outer curve of the beam so that the top edge of the tape coincides with the top edge of the beam on both sides of point to determine the baseline for point measurement. Record point lengths in appropriate blanks.

H-1-2-3-4. Circumferences are taken as detailed in illustration for each measurement. If brow point is missing, take H-1 and H-2 at smallest place between burr and G-2. If G-3 is missing, take H-3 halfway between the base and tip of G-2. If G-4 is missing, take H-4 halfway between G-2 and tip of main beam.

ENTRY AFFIDAVIT FOR ALL HUNTER-TAKEN TROPHIES

For the purpose of entry into the Boone and Crockett Club's® records, North American big game harvested by the use of the following methods or under the following conditions are ineligible:

I. Spotting or herding game from the air, followed by landing in its vicinity for the purpose of pursuit and shooting;
II. Herding or chasing with the aid of any motorized equipment;
III. Use of electronic communication devices, artificial lighting, or electronic light intensifying devices;
IV. Confined by artificial barriers, including escape-proof fenced enclosures;
V. Transplanted for the purpose of commercial shooting;
VI. By the use of traps or pharmaceuticals;
VII. While swimming, helpless in deep snow, or helpless in any other natural or artificial medium;
VIII. On another hunter's license;
IX. Not in full compliance with the game laws or regulations of the federal government or of any state, province, territory, or tribal council on reservations or tribal lands;

I certify that the trophy scored on this chart was not taken in violation of the conditions listed above. In signing this statement, I understand that if the information provided on this entry is found to be misrepresented or fraudulent in any respect, it will not be accepted into the Awards Program and 1) all of my prior entries are subject to deletion from future editions of **Records of North American Big Game** 2) future entries may not be accepted.

FAIR CHASE, as defined by the Boone and Crockett Club®, is the ethical, sportsmanlike and lawful pursuit and taking of any free-ranging wild, native North American big game animal in a manner that does not give the hunter an improper advantage over such game animals.

The Boone and Crockett Club® may exclude the entry of any animal that it deems to have been taken in an unethical manner or under conditions deemed inappropriate by the Club.

Date:_____ Signature of Hunter:_____
                                              (SIGNATURE MUST BE WITNESSED BY AN OFFICIAL MEASURER OR A NOTARY PUBLIC.)

Date:_____ Signature of Notary or Official Measurer:_____

Records of
North American
Big Game

250 Station Drive
Missoula, MT 59801
(406) 542-1888

BOONE AND CROCKETT CLUB®
OFFICIAL SCORING SYSTEM FOR NORTH AMERICAN BIG GAME TROPHIES

MINIMUM SCORES
AWARDS   ALL-TIME
360   375

TYPICAL
AMERICAN ELK (WAPITI)

Detail of Point
Measurement

Abnormal Points	
Right Antler	Left Antler
SUBTOTALS	
TOTAL TO E	

SEE OTHER SIDE FOR INSTRUCTIONS			COLUMN 1	COLUMN 2	COLUMN 3	COLUMN 4
A. No. Points on Right Antler	No. Points on Left Antler		Spread Credit	Right Antler	Left Antler	Difference
B. Tip to Tip Spread	C. Greatest Spread					
D. Inside Spread of Main Beams	SPREAD CREDIT MAY EQUAL BUT NOT EXCEED LONGER MAIN BEAM					
E. Total of Lengths of Abnormal Points						
F. Length of Main Beam						
G-1. Length of First Point						
G-2. Length of Second Point						
G-3. Length of Third Point						
G-4. Length of Fourth Point						
G-5. Length of Fifth Point						
G-6. Length of Sixth Point, If Present						
G-7. Length of Seventh Point, If Present						
H-1. Circumference at Smallest Place Between First and Second Points						
H-2. Circumference at Smallest Place Between Second and Third Points						
H-3. Circumference at Smallest Place Between Third and Fourth Points						
H-4. Circumference at Smallest Place Between Fourth and Fifth Points						
		TOTALS				

ADD	Column 1		Exact Locality Where Killed:	
	Column 2		Date Killed:	Hunter:
	Column 3		Owner:	Telephone #:
	Subtotal		Owner's Address:	
SUBTRACT Column 4			Guide's Name and Address:	
FINAL SCORE			Remarks: (Mention Any Abnormalities or Unique Qualities)	OM I.D. Number

I, _____ , certify that I have measured this trophy on _____
                 PRINT NAME   MM/DD/YYYYY

at _____
   STREET ADDRESS   CITY   STATE/PROVINCE

and that these measurements and data are, to the best of my knowledge and belief, made in accordance with the instructions given.

Witness: _____ Signature: _____ I.D. Number
                                           B&C OFFICIAL MEASURER

INSTRUCTIONS FOR MEASURING TYPICAL AMERICAN ELK (WAPITI)

All measurements must be made with a 1/4-inch wide flexible steel tape to the nearest one-eighth of an inch. (Note: A flexible steel cable can be used to measure points and main beams only.) Enter fractional figures in eighths, without reduction. Official measurements cannot be taken until the antlers have air dried for at least 60 days after the animal was killed.

  A. Number of Points on Each Antler: To be counted a point, the projection must be at least one inch long, with length exceeding width at one inch or more of length. All points are measured from tip of point to nearest edge of beam as illustrated. Beam tip is counted as a point but not measured as a point.

  B. Tip to Tip Spread is measured between tips of main beams.

  C. Greatest Spread is measured between perpendiculars at a right angle to the center line of the skull at widest part, whether across main beams or points.

  D. Inside Spread of Main Beams is measured at a right angle to the center line of the skull at widest point between main beams. Enter this measurement again as the Spread Credit I f it is less than or equal to the length of the longer main beam; if greater, enter longer main beam length for Spread Credit.

  E. Total of Lengths of all Abnormal Points: Abnormal Points are those non-typical in location (such as points originating from a point or from bottom or sides of main beam) or pattern (extra points, not generally paired). Measure in usual manner and record in appropriate blanks.

  F. Length of Main Beam is measured from the center of the lowest outside edge of burr over the outer side to the most distant point of the main beam. The point of beginning is that point on the burr where the center line along the outer side of the beam intersects the burr, then following generally the line of the illustration.

  G-1-2-3-4-5-6-7. Length of Normal Points: Normal points project from the top or front of the main beam in the general pattern illustrated. They are measured from nearest edge of main beam over outer curve to tip. Lay the tape along the outer curve of the beam so that the top edge of the tape coincides with the top edge of the beam on both sides of point to determine the baseline for point measurement. Record point length in appropriate blanks.

  H-1-2-3-4. Circumferences are taken as detailed in illustration for each measurement.

ENTRY AFFIDAVIT FOR ALL HUNTER-TAKEN TROPHIES

For the purpose of entry into the Boone and Crockett Club's® records, North American big game harvested by the use of the following methods or under the following conditions are ineligible:

    I.   Spotting or herding game from the air, followed by landing in its vicinity for the purpose of pursuit and shooting;
    II. Herding or chasing with the aid of any motorized equipment;
    III. Use of electronic communication devices, artificial lighting, or electronic light intensifying devices;
    IV. Confined by artificial barriers, including escape-proof fenced enclosures;
    V. Transplanted for the purpose of commercial shooting;
    VI. By the use of traps or pharmaceuticals;
    VII. While swimming, helpless in deep snow, or helpless in any other natural or artificial medium;
    VIII. On another hunter's license;
    IX. Not in full compliance with the game laws or regulations of the federal government or of any state, province, territory, or tribal council on reservations or tribal lands;

I certify that the trophy scored on this chart was not taken in violation of the conditions listed above. In signing this statement, I understand that if the information provided on this entry is found to be misrepresented or fraudulent in any respect, it will not be accepted into the Awards Program and 1) all of my prior entries are subject to deletion from future editions of **Records of North American Big Game** 2) future entries may not be accepted.

FAIR CHASE, as defined by the Boone and Crockett Club®, is the ethical, sportsmanlike and lawful pursuit and taking of any free-ranging wild, native North American big game animal in a manner that does not give the hunter an improper advantage over such game animals.

The Boone and Crockett Club® may exclude the entry of any animal that it deems to have been taken in an unethical manner or under conditions deemed inappropriate by the Club.

Date: _____ Signature of Hunter: _____
                                        (SIGNATURE MUST BE WITNESSED BY AN OFFICIAL MEASURER OR A NOTARY PUBLIC.)

Date: _____ Signature of Notary or Official Measurer: _____

Records of
North American
Big Game

250 Station Drive
Missoula, MT 59801
(406) 542-1888

BOONE AND CROCKETT CLUB®
OFFICIAL SCORING SYSTEM FOR NORTH AMERICAN BIG GAME TROPHIES

MINIMUM SCORES
AWARDS ALL-TIME
385   385

**NON-TYPICAL
AMERICAN ELK (WAPITI)**

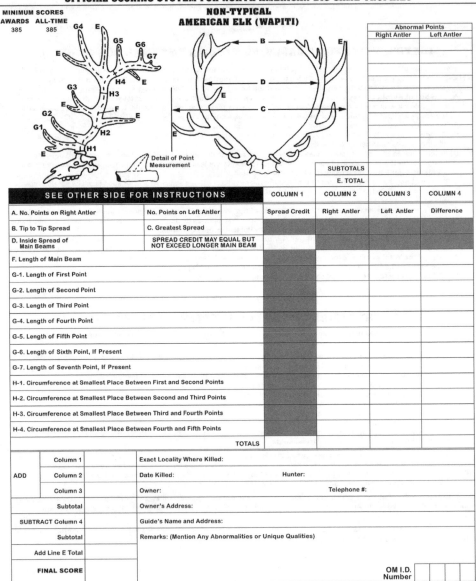

Abnormal Points	
Right Antler	Left Antler
SUBTOTALS	
E. TOTAL	

SEE OTHER SIDE FOR INSTRUCTIONS				COLUMN 1	COLUMN 2	COLUMN 3	COLUMN 4
A. No. Points on Right Antler		No. Points on Left Antler		Spread Credit	Right Antler	Left Antler	Difference
B. Tip to Tip Spread		C. Greatest Spread					
D. Inside Spread of Main Beams		SPREAD CREDIT MAY EQUAL BUT NOT EXCEED LONGER MAIN BEAM					
F. Length of Main Beam							
G-1. Length of First Point							
G-2. Length of Second Point							
G-3. Length of Third Point							
G-4. Length of Fourth Point							
G-5. Length of Fifth Point							
G-6. Length of Sixth Point, If Present							
G-7. Length of Seventh Point, If Present							
H-1. Circumference at Smallest Place Between First and Second Points							
H-2. Circumference at Smallest Place Between Second and Third Points							
H-3. Circumference at Smallest Place Between Third and Fourth Points							
H-4. Circumference at Smallest Place Between Fourth and Fifth Points							
			TOTALS				

ADD	Column 1		Exact Locality Where Killed:	
	Column 2		Date Killed:	Hunter:
	Column 3		Owner:	Telephone #:
	Subtotal		Owner's Address:	
SUBTRACT Column 4			Guide's Name and Address:	
	Subtotal		Remarks: (Mention Any Abnormalities or Unique Qualities)	
	Add Line E Total			
	FINAL SCORE			OM I.D. Number

Detail of Point Measurement

I, _____ , certify that I have measured this trophy on _____
PRINT NAME   MM/DD/YYYYY

at _____
STREET ADDRESS   CITY   STATE/PROVINCE

and that these measurements and data are, to the best of my knowledge and belief, made in accordance with the instructions given.

Witness: _____ Signature: _____ I.D. Number
B&C OFFICIAL MEASURER

INSTRUCTIONS FOR MEASURING NON-TYPICAL AMERICAN ELK (WAPITI)

All measurements must be made with a 1/4-inch wide flexible steel tape to the nearest one-eighth of an inch. (Note: A flexible steel cable can be used to measure points and main beams only.) Enter fractional figures in eighths, without reduction. Official measurements cannot be taken until the antlers have air dried for at least 60 days after the animal was killed.

A. Number of Points on Each Antler: To be counted a point, the projection must be at least one inch long, with length exceeding width at one inch or more of length. All points are measured from tip of point to nearest edge of beam as illustrated. Beam tip is counted as a point but not measured as a point.

B. Tip to Tip Spread is measured between tips of main beams.

C. Greatest Spread is measured between perpendiculars at a right angle to the center line of the skull at widest part, whether across main beams or points.

D. Inside Spread of Main Beams is measured at a right angle to the center line of the skull at widest point between main beams. Enter this measurement again as the Spread Credit if it is less than or equal to the length of the longer main beam; if greater, enter longer main beam length for Spread Credit.

E. Total of Lengths of all Abnormal Points: Abnormal Points are those non-typical in location (such as points originating from a point or from bottom or sides of main beam) or pattern (extra points, not generally paired). Measure in usual manner and record in appropriate blanks.

F. Length of Main Beam is measured from the center of the lowest outside edge of burr over the outer side to the most distant point of the main beam. The point of beginning is that point on the burr where the center line along the outer side of the beam intersects the burr, then following generally the line of the illustration.

G-1-2-3-4-5-6-7. Length of Normal Points: Normal points project from the top or front of the main beam in the general pattern illustrated. They are measured from nearest edge of main beam over outer curve to tip. Lay the tape along the outer curve of the beam so that the top edge of the tape coincides with the top edge of the beam on both sides of point to determine the baseline for point measurement. Record point length in appropriate blanks.

H-1-2-3-4. Circumferences are taken as detailed in illustration for each measurement.

ENTRY AFFIDAVIT FOR ALL HUNTER-TAKEN TROPHIES

For the purpose of entry into the Boone and Crockett Club's® records, North American big game harvested by the use of the following methods or under the following conditions are ineligible:

I. Spotting or herding game from the air, followed by landing in its vicinity for the purpose of pursuit and shooting;
II. Herding or chasing with the aid of any motorized equipment;
III. Use of electronic communication devices, artificial lighting, or electronic light intensifying devices;
IV. Confined by artificial barriers, including escape-proof fenced enclosures;
V. Transplanted for the purpose of commercial shooting;
VI. By the use of traps or pharmaceuticals;
VII. While swimming, helpless in deep snow, or helpless in any other natural or artificial medium;
VIII. On another hunter's license;
IX. Not in full compliance with the game laws or regulations of the federal government or of any state, province, territory, or tribal council on reservations or tribal lands;

I certify that the trophy scored on this chart was not taken in violation of the conditions listed above. In signing this statement, I understand that if the information provided on this entry is found to be misrepresented or fraudulent in any respect, it will not be accepted into the Awards Program and 1) all of my prior entries are subject to deletion from future editions of **Records of North American Big Game** 2) future entries may not be accepted.

FAIR CHASE, as defined by the Boone and Crockett Club®, is the ethical, sportsmanlike and lawful pursuit and taking of any free-ranging wild, native North American big game animal in a manner that does not give the hunter an improper advantage over such game animals.

The Boone and Crockett Club® may exclude the entry of any animal that it deems to have been taken in an unethical manner or under conditions deemed inappropriate by the Club.

Date:_____ Signature of Hunter:_____
(SIGNATURE MUST BE WITNESSED BY AN OFFICIAL MEASURER OR A NOTARY PUBLIC.)

Date:_____ Signature of Notary or Official Measurer:_____

Records of
North American
Big Game

250 Station Drive
Missoula, MT 59801
(406) 542-1888

BOONE AND CROCKETT CLUB®
OFFICIAL SCORING SYSTEM FOR NORTH AMERICAN BIG GAME TROPHIES

ROOSEVELT'S AND TULE ELK

MINIMUM SCORES		
	AWARDS	ALL-TIME
Roosevelt's	275	290
Tule	270	285

KIND OF ELK (check one)
☐ Roosevelt's
☐ Tule

Crown Points	
Right Antler	Left Antler

I. Crown Points Total

Abnormal Points	
Right Antler	Left Antler

Detail of Point
Measurement

TOTAL TO E

SEE OTHER SIDE FOR INSTRUCTIONS		COLUMN 1	COLUMN 2	COLUMN 3	COLUMN 4
A. No. Points on Right Antler	No. Points on Left Antler	Spread Credit	Right Antler	Left Antler	Difference
B. Tip to Tip Spread	C. Greatest Spread				
D. Inside Spread of Main Beams	SPREAD CREDIT MAY EQUAL BUT NOT EXCEED LONGER MAIN BEAM				
E. Total of Lengths of Abnormal Points					
F. Length of Main Beam					
G-1. Length of First Point					
G-2. Length of Second Point					
G-3. Length of Third Point					
G-4. Length of Fourth Point					
G-5. Length of Fifth Point					
G-6. Length of Sixth Point, If Present					
G-7. Length of Seventh Point, If Present					
H-1. Circumference at Smallest Place Between First and Second Points					
H-2. Circumference at Smallest Place Between Second and Third Points					
H-3. Circumference at Smallest Place Between Third and Fourth Points					
H-4. Circumference at Smallest Place Between Fourth and Fifth Points					
	TOTALS				

ADD	Column 1		Exact Locality Where Killed:
	Column 2		Date Killed: Hunter:
	Column 3		Owner: Telephone #:
	Total of I		Owner's Address:
	Subtotal		Guide's Name and Address:
SUBTRACT Column 4			Remarks: (Mention Any Abnormalities or Unique Qualities)
FINAL SCORE			OM I.D. Number

I, _____ , certify that I have measured this trophy on _____

PRINT NAME   MM/DD/YYYYY

at _____

STREET ADDRESS   CITY   STATE/PROVINCE

and that these measurements and data are, to the best of my knowledge and belief, made in accordance with the instructions given.

Witness: _____ Signature: _____ I.D. Number [ ][ ][ ][ ]

B&C OFFICIAL MEASURER

INSTRUCTIONS FOR MEASURING ROOSEVELT'S AND TULE ELK

All measurements must be made with a 1/4-inch wide flexible steel tape to the nearest one-eighth of an inch. (Note: A flexible steel cable can be used to measure points and main beams only.) Enter fractional figures in eighths, without reduction. Official measurements cannot be taken until the antlers have air dried for at least 60 days after the animal was killed.

A. Number of Points on Each Antler: to be counted a point, the projection must be at least one inch long, with length exceeding width at one inch or more of length. All points are measured from tip of point to nearest edge of beam as illustrated. Beam tip is counted as a point but not measured as a point.

B. Tip to Tip Spread is measured between tips of main beams.

C. Greatest Spread is measured between perpendiculars at a right angle to the center line of the skull at widest part, whether across main beams or points.

D. Inside Spread of Main Beams is measured at a right angle to the center line of the skull at widest point between main beams. Enter this measurement again as the Spread Credit if it is less than or equal to the length of the longer main beam; if greater, enter longer main beam length for Spread Credit.

E. Total of Lengths of all Abnormal Points: Abnormal Points are those non-typical in location or pattern occurring below G-4. Measure in usual manner and record in appropriate blanks. **Note: do not confuse with Crown Points that may occur in the vicinity of G-4, G-5, G-6, etc.**

F. Length of Main Beam is measured from the center of the lowest outside edge of burr over the outer side to the most distant point of the main beam. The point of beginning is that point on the burr where the center line along the outer side of the beam intersects the burr, then following generally the line of the illustration.

G-1-2-3-4-5-6-7. Length of Normal Points: Normal points project from the top or front of the main beam in the general pattern illustrated. They are measured from nearest edge of main beam over outer curve to tip. Lay the tape along the outer curve of the beam so that the top edge of the tape coincides with the top edge of the beam on both sides of point to determine the baseline for point measurement. Record point length in appropriate blanks.

H-1-2-3-4. Circumferences are taken as detailed in illustration for each measurement.

I. Crown Points: From the well-defined Royal on out to end of beam, all points other than the normal points in their typical locations are Crown Points. This includes points occurring on the Royal, on other normal points, on Crown Points, and on the bottom and sides of main beam after the Royal. Measure and record in appropriate blanks provided and add to score below.

ENTRY AFFIDAVIT FOR ALL HUNTER-TAKEN TROPHIES

For the purpose of entry into the Boone and Crockett Club's® records, North American big game harvested by the use of the following methods or under the following conditions are ineligible:

   I.   Spotting or herding game from the air, followed by landing in its vicinity for the purpose of pursuit and shooting;

   II. Herding or chasing with the aid of any motorized equipment;

  III. Use of electronic communication devices, artificial lighting, or electronic light intensifying devices;

  IV. Confined by artificial barriers, including escape-proof fenced enclosures;

   V. Transplanted for the purpose of commercial shooting;

  VI. By the use of traps or pharmaceuticals;

 VII. While swimming, helpless in deep snow, or helpless in any other natural or artificial medium;

VIII. On another hunter's license;

  IX. Not in full compliance with the game laws or regulations of the federal government or of any state, province, territory, or tribal council on reservations or tribal lands;

I certify that the trophy scored on this chart was not taken in violation of the conditions listed above. In signing this statement, I understand that if the information provided on this entry is found to be misrepresented or fraudulent in any respect, it will not be accepted into the Awards Program and 1) all of my prior entries are subject to deletion from future editions of **Records of North American Big Game** 2) future entries may not be accepted.

FAIR CHASE, as defined by the Boone and Crockett Club®, is the ethical, sportsmanlike and lawful pursuit and taking of any free-ranging wild, native North American big game animal in a manner that does not give the hunter an improper advantage over such game animals.

The Boone and Crockett Club® may exclude the entry of any animal that it deems to have been taken in an unethical manner or under conditions deemed inappropriate by the Club.

Date: _____ Signature of Hunter: _____

(SIGNATURE MUST BE WITNESSED BY AN OFFICIAL MEASURER OR A NOTARY PUBLIC.)

Date: _____ Signature of Notary or Official Measurer: _____

Records of
North American
Big Game

250 Station Drive
Missoula, MT 59801
(406) 542-1888

BOONE AND CROCKETT CLUB®
OFFICIAL SCORING SYSTEM FOR NORTH AMERICAN BIG GAME TROPHIES

CARIBOU

	MINIMUM SCORES	
	AWARDS	ALL-TIME
mountain	360	390
woodland	265	295
barren ground	375	400
Central Canada		
barren ground	345	360
Quebec-Labrador	365	375

KIND OF CARIBOU (check one)

☐ mountain
☐ woodland
☐ barren ground
☐ Central Canada
   barren ground
☐ Quebec-Labrador

Detail of Point
Measurement

SEE OTHER SIDE FOR INSTRUCTIONS			COLUMN 1	COLUMN 2	COLUMN 3	COLUMN 4
A. Tip to Tip Spread			Spread Credit	Right Antler	Left Antler	Difference
B. Greatest Spread						
C. Inside Spread of Main Beams		SPREAD CREDIT MAY EQUAL BUT NOT EXCEED LONGER MAIN BEAM				
D. Number of Points on Each Antler Excluding Brows						
Number of Points on Each Brow						
E. Length of Main Beam						
F-1. Length of Brow Palm or First Point						
F-2. Length of Bez or Second Point						
F-3. Length of Rear Point, If Present						
F-4. Length of Second Longest Top Point						
F-5. Length of Longest Top Point						
G-1. Width of Brow Palm						
G-2. Width of Top Palm						
H-1. Circumference at Smallest Place Between Brow and Bez Point						
H-2. Circumference at Smallest Place Between Bez and Rear Point						
H-3. Circumference at Smallest Place Between Rear Point and First Top Point						
H-4. Circumference at Smallest Place Between Two Longest Top Palm Points						
		TOTALS				

ADD	Column 1		Exact Locality Where Killed:	
	Column 2		Date Killed:	Hunter:
	Column 3		Owner:	Telephone #:
	Subtotal		Owner's Address:	
SUBTRACT Column 4			Guide's Name and Address:	
FINAL SCORE			Remarks: (Mention Any Abnormalities or Unique Qualities)	OM I.D. Number

I, _____ , certify that I have measured this trophy on _____
　　　　　　PRINT NAME　　　　　　　　　　　　　　　　　　　　　　　　　　　　　　　　　MM/DD/YYYYY

at _____
　　STREET ADDRESS　　　　　　　　　　　　　　　　　　　　　　　　　CITY　　　　　　　　　　　　　　STATE/PROVINCE

and that these measurements and data are, to the best of my knowledge and belief, made in accordance with the instructions given.

Witness: _____ Signature: _____ I.D. Number [　] [　] [　] [　]
　　　　　　　　　　　　　　　　　　　　　　　　　　　　B&C OFFICIAL MEASURER

INSTRUCTIONS FOR MEASURING CARIBOU

All measurements must be made with a 1/4-inch wide flexible steel tape to the nearest one-eighth of an inch. (Note: A flexible steel cable can be used to measure points and main beams only.) Enter fractional figures in eighths, without reduction. Official measurements cannot be taken until the antlers have air dried for at least 60 days after the animal was killed.

A. Tip to Tip Spread is measured between tips of main beams.

B. Greatest Spread is measured between perpendiculars at a right angle to the center line of the skull at widest part, whether across main beams or points.

C. Inside Spread of Main Beams is measured at a right angle to the center line of the skull at widest point between main beams. Enter this measurement again as the Spread Credit if it is less than or equal to the length of the longer main beam; if greater, enter longer main beam length for Spread Credit.

D. Number of Points on Each Antler: To be counted a point, a projection must be at least one-half inch long, with length exceeding width at one-half inch or more of length. Beam tip is counted as a point but not measured as a point. There are no "abnormal" points in caribou.

E. Length of Main Beam is measured from the center of the lowest outside edge of burr over the outer side to the most distant point of the main beam. The point of beginning is that point on the burr where the center line along the outer side of the beam intersects the burr, then following generally the line of the illustration.

F-1-2-3. Length of Points are measured from nearest edge of beam over outer curve to tip. Lay the tape along the outer curve of the beam so that the top edge of the tape coincides with the top edge of the beam on both sides of point to determine the baseline for point measurement. Record point lengths in appropriate blanks.

F-4-5. Length of Points are measured from the tip of the point to the top of the beam, then at a right angle to the bottom edge of beam. The Second Longest Top Point **cannot** be a point branch of the Longest Top Point.

G-1. Width of Brow is measured in a straight line from top edge to lower edge, as illustrated, with measurement line at a right angle to main axis of brow.

G-2. Width of Top Palm is measured from midpoint of lower edge of main beam to midpoint of a dip between points, at widest part of palm. The line of measurement begins and ends at midpoints of palm edges, which gives credit for palm thickness.

H-1-2-3-4. Circumferences are taken as illustrated for measurements. If brow point is missing, take H-1 at smallest point between burr and bez point. If rear point is missing, take H-2 and H-3 measurements at smallest place between bez and first top point. Do not depress the tape into any dips of the palm or main beam.

ENTRY AFFIDAVIT FOR ALL HUNTER-TAKEN TROPHIES

For the purpose of entry into the Boone and Crockett Club's® records, North American big game harvested by the use of the following methods or under the following conditions are ineligible:

I. Spotting or herding game from the air, followed by landing in its vicinity for the purpose of pursuit and shooting;
II. Herding or chasing with the aid of any motorized equipment;
III. Use of electronic communication devices, artificial lighting, or electronic light intensifying devices;
IV. Confined by artificial barriers, including escape-proof fenced enclosures;
V. Transplanted for the purpose of commercial shooting;
VI. By the use of traps or pharmaceuticals;
VII. While swimming, helpless in deep snow, or helpless in any other natural or artificial medium;
VIII. On another hunter's license;
IX. Not in full compliance with the game laws or regulations of the federal government or of any state, province, territory, or tribal council on reservations or tribal lands;

I certify that the trophy scored on this chart was not taken in violation of the conditions listed above. In signing this statement, I understand that if the information provided on this entry is found to be misrepresented or fraudulent in any respect, it will not be accepted into the Awards Program and 1) all of my prior entries are subject to deletion from future editions of **Records of North American Big Game** 2) future entries may not be accepted.

FAIR CHASE, as defined by the Boone and Crockett Club®, is the ethical, sportsmanlike and lawful pursuit and taking of any free-ranging wild, native North American big game animal in a manner that does not give the hunter an improper advantage over such game animals.

The Boone and Crockett Club® may exclude the entry of any animal that it deems to have been taken in an unethical manner or under conditions deemed inappropriate by the Club.

Date: _____ Signature of Hunter: _____
　　　　　　　　　　　　　　　　　(SIGNATURE MUST BE WITNESSED BY AN OFFICIAL MEASURER OR A NOTARY PUBLIC.)

Date: _____ Signature of Notary or Official Measurer: _____

Records of
North American
Big Game

250 Station Drive
Missoula, MT 59801
(406) 542-1888

BOONE AND CROCKETT CLUB®
OFFICIAL SCORING SYSTEM FOR NORTH AMERICAN BIG GAME TROPHIES

MOOSE

MINIMUM SCORES	AWARDS	ALL-TIME
Canada	185	195
Alaska-Yukon	210	224
Wyoming	140	155

KIND OF MOOSE (check one)
- ☐ Canada
- ☐ Alaska-Yukon
- ☐ Wyoming

Detail of Point
Measurement

	Abnormal Points	
	Right Antler	Left Antler
NUMBER OF POINTS		
TOTAL TO B.		

SEE OTHER SIDE FOR INSTRUCTIONS	COLUMN 1	COLUMN 2	COLUMN 3	COLUMN 4
		Right Antler	Left Antler	Difference
A. Greatest Spread				
B. Number of Abnormal Points on Both Antlers				
C. Number of Normal Points				
D. Width of Palm				
E. Length of Palm Including Brow Palm				
F. Circumference of Beam at Smallest Place				
TOTALS				

ADD	Column 1		Exact Locality Where Killed:
	Column 2		Date Killed: Hunter:
	Column 3		Owner: Telephone #:
	Subtotal		Owner's Address:
SUBTRACT Column 4			Guide's Name and Address:
FINAL SCORE			Remarks: (Mention Any Abnormalities or Unique Qualities)

I, _____ , certify that I have measured this trophy on _____
PRINT NAME   MM/DD/YYYYY

at _____
STREET ADDRESS   CITY   STATE/PROVINCE

and that these measurements and data are, to the best of my knowledge and belief, made in accordance with the instructions given.

Witness: _____ Signature: _____ I.D. Number ☐☐☐☐
                                        B&C OFFICIAL MEASURER

INSTRUCTIONS FOR MEASURING MOOSE

Measurements must be made with a 1/4-inch wide flexible steel tape to the nearest one-eighth of an inch. Enter fractional figures in eighths, without reduction. Official measurements cannot be taken until antlers have air dried for at least 60 days after animal was killed.

A. **Greatest Spread** is measured between perpendiculars in a straight line at a right angle to the center line of the skull.

B. **Number of Abnormal Points on Both Antlers:** Abnormal points are those projections originating from normal points or from the upper or lower palm surface, or from the inner edge of palm (see illustration). Abnormal points must be at least one inch long, with length exceeding width at one inch or more of length.

C. **Number of Normal Points:** Normal points originate from the outer edge of palm. To be counted a point, a projection must be at least one inch long, with the length exceeding width at one inch or more of length. Be sure to verify whether or not each projection qualifies as a point.

D. **Width of Palm** is taken in contact with the under surface of palm, at a right angle to the inner edge of palm. The line of measurement should begin and end at the midpoint of the palm edge, which gives credit for the desirable character of palm thickness.

E. **Length of Palm** including Brow Palm is taken in contact with the surface along the underside of the palm, **parallel** to the inner edge, from dips between points at the top to dips between points at the bottom. If a bay is present, measure across the open bay if the proper line of measurement, parallel to **inner edge**, follows this path. The line of measurement should begin and end at the midpoint of the palm edge, which gives credit for the desirable character of palm thickness.

F. **Circumference** of Beam at Smallest Place is taken as illustrated.

ENTRY AFFIDAVIT FOR ALL HUNTER-TAKEN TROPHIES

For the purpose of entry into the Boone and Crockett Club's® records, North American big game harvested by the use of the following methods or under the following conditions are ineligible:

I. Spotting or herding game from the air, followed by landing in its vicinity for the purpose of pursuit and shooting;

II. Herding or chasing with the aid of any motorized equipment;

III. Use of electronic communication devices, artificial lighting, or electronic light intensifying devices;

IV. Confined by artificial barriers, including escape-proof fenced enclosures;

V. Transplanted for the purpose of commercial shooting;

VI. By the use of traps or pharmaceuticals;

VII. While swimming, helpless in deep snow, or helpless in any other natural or artificial medium;

VIII. On another hunter's license;

IX. Not in full compliance with the game laws or regulations of the federal government or of any state, province, territory, or tribal council on reservations or tribal lands;

I certify that the trophy scored on this chart was not taken in violation of the conditions listed above. In signing this statement, I understand that if the information provided on this entry is found to be misrepresented or fraudulent in any respect, it will not be accepted into the Awards Program and 1) all of my prior entries are subject to deletion from future editions of **Records of North American Big Game** 2) future entries may not be accepted.

FAIR CHASE, as defined by the Boone and Crockett Club®, is the ethical, sportsmanlike and lawful pursuit and taking of any free-ranging wild, native North American big game animal in a manner that does not give the hunter an improper advantage over such game animals.

The Boone and Crockett Club® may exclude the entry of any animal that it deems to have been taken in an unethical manner or under conditions deemed inappropriate by the Club.

Date: _____ Signature of Hunter: _____

(SIGNATURE MUST BE WITNESSED BY AN OFFICIAL MEASURER OR A NOTARY PUBLIC.)

Date: _____ Signature of Notary or Official Measurer: _____